THE CONSERVATION OF
EUROPEAN BATS

R.E. Stebbings

With the assistance of the IUCN/SSC
Chiroptera Specialist Group

CHRISTOPHER HELM
London

© 1988 R.E. Stebbings
Christopher Helm (Publishers) Ltd, Imperial House,
21-25 North Street, Bromley, Kent BR1 1SD

ISBN 0-7470-3013-8

A CIP catalogue record for this book
is available from the British Library

To Owen Gilbert,
who first kindled my passion
for the welfare of bats

 EUROPEAN YEAR
OF THE ENVIRONMENT

Printed and bound in Great Britain
by Biddles Ltd, Guildford, Surrey.

Contents

Table of Contents

Page

Foreword

There is a growing awareness of the need to ensure the survival of representative populations of wildlife throughout Europe. Plants and animals regarded as pests have usually been studied in detail and conservation of these is not often necessary. But of the other wildlife, while the attractive species such as orchids, birds and some mammals (for example otters and bison), have received a lot of attention, generally plants, insects, reptiles and bats have been neglected.

Since European Conservation Year in 1970, a rapidly increasing number of scientists and naturalists across Europe, have become aware of the need to protect bats.

Bats have an immense fascination for people. In the past it was often one of fear and superstition, but increasingly it is the wonder of these tiny animals; having the ability to fly, can have such a sophisticated life-style and an almost incredible capability to hunt food and migrate over long distances, all in darkness.

Unfortunately, this popular appeal of bats is only now developing and it is too late to prevent some species becoming locally extinct. Indeed, in those States lacking education programmes, this awakening has yet to happen. However, over a wide area there is now a strong desire to redress the balance and bats are beginning to benefit from protection and from conservation projects in many countries. The purpose of this book is to describe the problems together with some of the solutions already achieved; and, most importantly, to show what is needed to ensure bats remain for future generations to marvel at. Most of the goals being sought can be achieved with careful planning, but all must be realised if adequate populations of bats are to survive.

This book forms an action plan of the Chiroptera Specialist Group of the Species Survival Commission (SSC) of the International Union for the Conservation of Nature and Natural Resources (IUCN). The Chiroptera Specialist Group is one of over 80 groups of the SSC and draws upon the knowledge of the world's bat experts, who freely provide their time and scientific expertise. The major aim of the SSC is to prevent the extinction of species by finding solutions to conservation problems. The specialist groups advise how this might be done for their species. IUCN's major role is to co-ordinate and provide detailed guidance on a global programme of applied conservation. It encourages projects which equate the needs of man with the wise use of natural resources. Development and publication of a World Conservation Strategy in 1980 is a recipe to the World's nations, showing how this might be achieved.

Founded in 1948, IUCN is the world's largest, most representative and most experienced alliance of active conservation authorities, agencies and interest groups. Its more than 500 members include States, governmental departments and most of the leading independent conservation organisations, national and international.

Geographic Area

Europe has no precise boundaries and so an arbitrary line was selected at about longitude 27 degrees East, and countries to be included were chosen if over half their territory was west of that line. Thus, Finland (extending to 32 degrees East) is included, but Ukranian SSR (extending to 22 degrees East) is not. These show the maximum deviation from the line.

The Baltic Soviet Socialist Republics of Estonia, Latvia and Lithuania occur almost totally west of the selected longitude and their bat fauna is similar to those of Finland and Poland. Bats are known to migrate between those countries.

To the south, west and north of Europe, the natural boundaries are the Mediterranean Sea and the Atlantic and Arctic Oceans. However, arbitrary decisions had to be made as to which islands were to be included. Generally those islands with close political and physical links with mainland States are included, while small, isolated or independent islands are not. Therefore, included are Crete (Greece), Malta, Sardinia (Italy), Corsica (France) and the Balearic Isles (Spain). Excluded are the oceanic Azores and Madeira (Portugal), Canary Isles (Spain), Faroes and Svalbard (Denmark) and Iceland. The latter three islands have no resident bats, nor do the Shetland Isles (Great Britain). However, the Outer Hebrides and Orkney Isles do have at least one resident species of bat.

The only other European States lacking reports are Andorra, Monaco, San Marino, Vatican City and Liechtenstein.

The landmass being reported on, totals 4.95 million square kilometres, and the omission of the small mainland States amounts to 673 square kilometres.

Acknowledgements

The production of this action plan could not have happened without the letter writing, co-ordination, collation of information and word processing, often long into the night, by Sheila Walsh. Many thanks go to her as well as Henry Arnold, Tony Hutson, and Paul Racey, for their helpful criticism.

The Fauna and Flora Preservation Society, through John Burton, generously supported this project, and Simon Stuart (SSC, IUCN) also gave help and encouragement at all stages. I wish to thank the publishers Christopher Helm for all the assistance they provided, and Simon Hartley for drawing the maps.

I am especially grateful to all the following scientists and friends, who have most kindly provided papers, reports and translations. Without their generous help, the plan could not have been written. Any mistakes are entirely my responsibility and I herewith apologise to anyone if I have misrepresented any details in the country accounts. This conservation plan will evolve, and any faults will be corrected.

Belgium: J Fairon., **Bulgaria:** P Beron., **Channel Isles:** P Costen, B Carrol, M Romeril., **Czechoslovakia:** Z Bauerová, J Gaisler, P Rybár, J Zima., **Denmark:** H Baage., **Eire:** P O'Sullivan., **Estonia** SSR: M Masing., **Finland:** J Lokki, N Hagner, T Stjernberg., **France:** J Noblet., **Gibraltar:** M Waite., **Great Britain:** H R Arnold, S Lyster, A J Mitchell-Jones, P Oswald, D Roberts, A J Walsh., **Democratic Republic of Germany:** E Grimmberger, H Hackethal, A Schmidt, W Schober., **Federal Republic of Germany:** M Braun, U Jüdes, R Mohr, A Nagel, K Richarz, H Roer, H Merz., **Greece:** J G Iliopoulou-Georgudaki,

A Legakis., **Hungary:** G Topál., **Isle of Man:** M Boyde, L S Garrad., **Italy:** V Calandra, E Vernier., **Malta:** J Borg., **Netherlands:** G H Glas, P Lina, A M Voûte., **Norway:** I Byrkjedal, P O Syvertsen., **Poland:** T Kokurewicz, M Kowalski, A Krzanowski, G Lesinski, Z Urbanczyk, B W Woloszyn., **Portugal:** C Magalháes, J Palmeirim., **Romania:** P Barbu., **Spain:** J Benzal, J M de Benito, M Freán, E Moreno, S G Prieto, A Villarino., **Switzerland:** V Aellen, R Arlettaz, G Berthoud, J-D Blant, J Gebhard, C Huber, A Keller, Y Leuzinger, P Moeschler, T Sandoz, K Zbinden, P Zingg., **Sweden:** I Ahlén, R Gerell., Yugoslavia: B Dulic, B Kyrstufek.

Part One

Natural History of Bats:
Their Conservation Problems and Solutions

1

The Natural History of Bats

In order to appreciate fully the conservation problems facing bats, it is necessary to have an understanding of the way bats live. Indeed, without detailed knowledge of their biology, incorrect protective measures may be taken which accelerate their decline. Such errors already have been made, even to the extent of walling up a cave entrance to prevent people disturbing bats, resulting in bats dying because they could not get out to feed! That kind of problem is rare, but a common factor to many declines has been disturbance of bats, often by biologists studying them. It was Dutch biologists in the 1950s who first appreciated the harm their research caused to bats. With this realisation, they and biologists elsewhere subsequently tried to establish ways to gather information without harming the animals.

Bats belong to the order Chiroptera. Worldwide there are nearly 1,000 species, grouped into 19 families, but new species are being identified each year. European bats belong to three families; Rhinolophidae (five species), Vespertilionidae (24 species) and Molossidae (one species), all members of the suborder Microchiroptera.

These 30 species represent about 30 per cent of the native mammal fauna in Europe. As a group, bats have been neglected by biologists because of their secretive roosting habits and because they are nocturnal.

The first species to be studied were the conspicuous larger bats, *Myotis myotis* and *Rhinolophus ferrumequinum*, which often roosted in huge colonies in house roofs or in caves. Both these species suffered substantial declines, due to the research workers as well as other factors detailed in chapter two. These species are essentially cave dwelling.

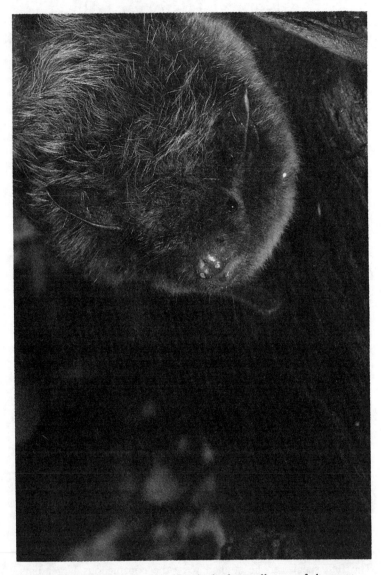

*Plate 1. Daubenton's bat, **Myotis daubentonii**, one of the most widespread species in Europe, whose population appears to be increasing in some areas in the north (photo: R. E. Stebbings).*

About half of Europe's bat species spend part of their lives roosting in caves, mostly in hibernation with some in nurseries. The other species are typically tree roosting, but almost all bats utilise man-made structures, especially buildings. Generally, relatively little is known about the 'tree' bats as they tend to form smaller colonies and are difficult to locate.

Colonies

Bats are mostly gregarious animals, some of which form the largest aggregations of any warm-blooded animals. A few tropical caves contain an estimated 50 million bats. In Romania, a cluster of 100,000 bats was estimated in one cave, whilst several countries in southern Europe are known to have caves containing many thousands of bats. Undoubtedly there will be a large number of substantial populations yet to be discovered amongst the tens of thousands of caves awaiting examination by biologists, especially around the Mediterranean. One previously unknown group of 60,000 *Miniopterus schreibersii* was recently discovered in a cave at the north east end of the Pyrenees in Aude, France.

In central and northern Europe, groups of over 1,000 bats are now rare, but there is some evidence of former colonies numbering many thousands. In Britain, in the last 30 years, a number of colonies were identified involving *R. ferrumequinum, Myotis nattereri,* and *Myotis daubentonii,* which formally were estimated each to contain over 10,000 animals. In northern Europe, by far the largest present known population is found in western Poland. It numbers well over 20,000 bats of eleven species.

'Colonies' and 'populations'

The last examples illustrate the different types of aggregations bats form. The term 'colony' refers to a group of bats of one species which normally associate and breed exclusively with one another. At some time of the year over half of all members of a colony may be in a single roost. By contrast, the tunnels in Poland shelter a 'population' of bats of many species, with individuals of each species gathering from many colonies. In the past the term 'colony' has often been used loosely to denote any group of two or more bats in one site.

Social Organisation

Little is known about the social organisation of bats in colonies. Seasonally they form groups of differing age and sex composition and there are some types of association common to all species. At all times of the year, bats of every species may roost individually or may form groups. The size of groups can change daily, even in winter. Frequently mother and offspring hibernate together many kilometres from the birth site. Little is known about the recognition of individuals by other bats, but it appears some bats may form life-long social groups.

Metabolism

Mammals are termed 'warm-blooded' because they generate heat in their bodies and regulate their temperature within set limits. Humans have a temperature of about 37 degrees Celsius which normally varies by only one degree. Bats in Europe, however, do not exhibit a more or less constant body temperature. Even on one summer's day they can range from 12 to 41 degrees Celsius. This is because bats are dependent on flying insects, a food source which, though high in energy, is very patchily distributed.

Flying insects may be one hundred-fold more plentiful on one night than on the next, owing mostly to weather conditions. A flying bat, hunting for insects uses large amounts of energy. If body temperature and hence energy consumption remained high while roosting, bats could not survive the periods of food shortage during cold or windy weather. To conserve energy during the day and at night when feeding is poor, bats allow their body temperature to drop and they become torpid. In winter bats need to remain in torpor for long periods due to the lack of insect food. However, there is a wide variation in the lengths of torpidity between species and throughout the range of individual species. For example, a species such as *P. pipistrellus* living in the extreme south of Italy, may be able to find some food on most winter nights, but the same species wintering in Poland or Sweden will rarely find much food.

Annual Behaviour Cycle

In spring, members of one colony gather in increasingly larger clusters consisting mainly of pregnant females with small numbers of immature bats. At parturition, virtually all pregnant females roost communally but drift away as the young are weaned. In summer, adult males and immature bats tend to roost in small groups, remaining in contact with the adult females by making transient visits to the nursery. By the autumn, dominant adult males of most species roost individually in traditional sites, to which they attract females for mating. This period merges into the hibernation phase. Within this general pattern there appears to be much variation but more detailed knowledge is required for many species.

Hibernation

Bats do not remain continuously torpid throughout winter. The frequency of natural awakenings varies according to species, sex, age, season, amount of food reserves and temperature of their roost. Essentially, those which roost at low temperatures arouse less frequently than those in warm surroundings. Although the purpose and mechanism is not fully understood, it is likely to involve the way bats re-adjust their internal chemical balance. Prior to hibernation, bats accumulate food reserves which can amount to one third of their body mass. Most of these reserves are fat and as this is metabolised, excess water as well as other, often toxic, wastes are produced in the body. Upon awakening, one of the first actions is to urinate. An arousal may not result in a bat moving position or flying, but grooming often ensues.

Bats select their environmental conditions carefully. The 'cave bats' choose temperatures which correlate closely with their energy stores and the season, while 'tree bats' tolerate widely fluctuating temperatures. For example, one experienced female *R. ferrumequinum* with a large reserve of fat, may begin hibernation deep in a cave showing no diurnal variation in ambient temperature, at 10.5 degrees Celsius. By February, the same bat may be found roosting at 8.5 degrees Celsius. In contrast *P. pipistrellus* may experience, without awakening, an ambient temperature change in 24 hours from minus five to plus 13 degrees Celsius.

Summer

At the end of hibernation, bats arouse more frequently and attempt to replace lost food reserves. Most species, when they return to the roost after feeding, cluster while digestion takes place, then they separate and cool quickly to conserve energy. Pregnant females often continue to cluster and maintain higher than ambient temperatures to enable foetal development to progress, but if food is scarce they too become torpid. This clustering allows more energy to be used for breeding, and less is wasted in keeping warm.

In late pregnancy the preferred roost temperature is about 30 degrees Celsius. In southern Europe, where mean annual temperatures exceed 14 degrees Celsius, nursery colonies of many species are found in caves. In central and northern areas, only large colonies can raise their young successfully in such places. These bats choose domes, often in the entrance parts of caves where warm air from outside may enter and be trapped. Also the body heat from clustered bats gathers in these domes. However, many former cave nurseries have disappeared, presumably because the colony size dwindled to the point where it became uneconomic or impossible for females to raise young successfully.

Adult males in summer remain torpid most of the time, only venturing out to feed when conditions are favourable. By late summer when their food reserves are high, they remain alert and active, but feeding little for about two months until just prior to hibernation. They loose a considerable amount of weight in this period, but rapidly make it up before hibernation.

*Plate 2. Pipistrelle, **Pipistrellus pipistrellus**, nursery colony, with one baby suckling from its mother (photo: R. E. Stebbings).*

Roosts

Bats can be found roosting almost anywhere, and they constantly investigate 'new' sites, which will be adopted if found suitable. Many of the most important bat roosts in Europe are man-made.

Bats do not always hang, indeed the *Rhinolophus* species are the only ones which exclusively hang. Most bats cannot be seen at any time because of their secretive habit of squeezing into crevices, with some, such as *M. daubentonii*, habitually crawling into loose scree sometimes up to a depth of one metre. In hibernation usually there is no clue as to where bats are roosting, except when trees are cut down or walls demolished. In some chalk mines, such as those in Jutland, Denmark, there are several thousand *M. daubentonii* known to be present, but virtually none can be seen for much of the winter. They emerge in early spring to hang on the walls for a period before leaving for the summer.

Before humans began building, bats lived mostly in hollow trees, rock crevices or caves. Some hang under leaves, behind loose bark on trees, amongst exposed tree roots and some use the burrows excavated by other animals.

All kinds of buildings have been adopted by bats. Any site giving seclusion and shelter may be used: tombs, churches, walls, bridges, castles and fortifications of all kinds, tunnels, mines of every variety, domestic buildings, cellars and ice houses. Amongst the most important roosts are thick walls, often built with facing stone or brick, but filled with loosely packed rubble. Bats crawl inside through narrow crevices often where cement has fallen out, and large numbers may be found amongst the rubble. Both 'cave' and 'tree' species exploit such places. Mines with vertical shafts, a metre in diameter and over 100 metres deep, present no difficulty to some species and large colonies have been found using such places. Also bats are known to land on roads to crawl through manhole covers and gratings, and to roost in culverts and sewers.

How many roosts does one bat use?

It is most unusual for a bat of any species to occupy the same roost throughout the year. Instead bats live in a variety of sites, each having differing characteristics. Choice of roost will depend on many factors, including its size, temperature regime and proximity to feeding grounds. Members of one colony of *R. ferrumequinum*, are known to occupy well over 100 roosts annually. These are distributed in an area of 2,500 square kilometres. Although many are used by only one or two bats for a few days, major clusters are found in others, containing 25 to 40 per cent of the colony, sometimes staying there for months.

Movements and Migrations

Individual bats may use roosts separated by distances of a few metres or hundreds of kilometres. However, movements between roosts follow seasonal patterns and are not haphazard wanderings.

The most obvious movements are between nurseries and hibernacula. Occasionally these are in the same general site, for example, different parts of the same building or, from entrances of caves to deep underground, but movements often involve bats travelling many kilometres.

Compared with birds, relatively few bats have been ringed. Nevertheless, long distance movements have been recorded. Some bats which spend the summer in northern countries such as Finland, Estonia, Poland and the Democratic Republic of Germany, are known to travel mostly in a south westerly direction to winter in southern France, Switzerland and other Mediterranean areas. Bats from the Netherlands were found several hundred kilometres away, in south and west France. Most of the long distance movements have involved *Nyctalus noctula, N. leisleri, Pipistrellus nathusii, P. pipistrellus* and *Vespertilio murinus*. However, many species are known to travel up to 100 kilometres from summer roosts, in order to find suitable hibernacula.

There is evidence to suggest some bats undertake long distance movements in periods of extreme cold, when it is believed their usual roosts become too cold. Severe winter weather in north east Europe, with strong east winds, has caused bats to fly west to countries bordering the North Sea. The significance of such movements is not known.

Reproduction and Longevity

Bats in Europe have adapted to the needs of adults meeting for mating, with subsequent parturition being timed to coincide with peak availability of food. In northern Europe, hibernation lasts up to seven months and because the weather in spring is often unpredictable and frequently cold, there are obvious advantages in mating before hibernation. This allows females to optimise their spring behaviour to ensure successful pregnancy.

All species mate predominantly in the autumn, but a few such as *M. daubentonii* continue throughout the winter. Having been inseminated, ovulation and fertilisation occurs immediately in *M. schreibersii*, but the ovum does not implant until the spring. This phenomenon of delayed implantation is well known amongst other mammals such as some deer, badgers and seals. In all other bat species the sperm is stored by the female until spring, when ovulation, fertilisation and implantation occurs. Delayed fertilisation is unique to insectivorous bats.

For all species, even after implantation, gestation does not take a predetermined time span, but rather its length depends primarily on food availability. Lack of food, especially in early pregnancy, causes bats to seek cool places to become torpid and foetal development is suspended.

All the pregnant females of one colony gather together in nurseries, and in southern Europe most births occur in late May or early June, with bats in the northern areas being about one month later.

Most species normally produce a single young, but *N. noctula* and *P. pipistrellus* often have twins. Young of most species grow quickly, being nearly full grown and beginning to fly after about three weeks. *N. noctula* and *Tadarida teniotis* usually do not fly until four or even five weeks old.

The young bats normally remain in a crèche at night when the mothers go to feed, but if roost conditions become unsuitable the mothers will carry their babies to a new roost.

Towards the end of weaning, females may live apart from their young during the day, but return at dusk, first to feed the young and then to take it out, presumably to show it how to find and catch food.

In southern Europe most Vespertilionidae mature in the first autumn and breed at the end of the first year. In northern Europe, some will breed in their first year and most of the rest in

*Plate 3. Brandt's bat, **Myotis brandtii**, a long overlooked species, finally identified as recently as 1971 and since found widely over much of central and northern Europe (photo: R. E. Stebbings).*

their second. The same pattern appears to be true for the small *Rhinolophus hipposideros*. In contrast female *R. ferrumequinum* in southern areas first breed in their second or third years, but in Great Britain most do not breed until they are in their fourth year and exceptionally a few individuals are at least seven years old before their first young is born.

Adult females of all species sometimes do not breed every year. This failure is probably related to the lack of food at critical times. Much more research is needed to establish the normal breeding patterns for all but a few species.

Mark and recapture studies have shown wild bats can live for over 30 years, although average life spans are about four to five years.

Populations

With an average annual fecundity rate of one or less, high survival of adult females is essential if populations are to thrive. A pregnant female makes a high investment in its offspring and in many years, overall juvenile survival to hibernation is well over 90 per cent. However, bad weather and lack of food can be disastrous if they coincide with lactation. If the mother's milk fails, the baby is abandoned and will die. Occasionally, whole colonies have left their young for this reason. Survival rate appears to be higher in the larger colonies, a feature probably related to the improved energy economy achieved by the larger clusters.

Sex ratio at birth is usually unity, but some studies have shown a significant male bias in small colonies whose size is in decline.

Habitats and Food

Although knowledge of many aspects of bat natural history is poor, worse is our comprehension of what habitats each species needs. We do know species such as *Myotis dasycneme* and *M. daubentonii* are observed over water, and that *Tadarida* and *Nyctalus* bats fly fast and high, well clear of obstacles, but at present we can do little more than describe where bats are found and some of what they eat.

Analysis both of flying insects and what can be identified in bat droppings can give an indication of the relative importance of prey species in bats' diet, and which particular habitats are favoured.

Deciduous woodland, scrub, old pasture, marshland and open water are all known to be vital elements in providing a rich and abundant supply of insects in places for bats to hunt. Old and hollow trees are especially valuable, because of the food and shelter they provide. Only now are studies begining, to investigate the details of habitat and food requirements for bats.

Research and Survey Techniques

Much useful work can be achieved by watching entrances to roosts, counting emerging bats and recording weather details. There is an urgent need to locate colonies, estimate population sizes and monitor such places over a long period so changes in distribution or status will be detected. Counting bats inside roosts is essential, but it must be done carefully both in summer and winter. Caves in southern Europe have been greatly neglected, and large, important populations occur there.

There is also a need for more detailed research on the population ecology of representative species in differing climatic zones. These projects require careful planning to avoid damaging the populations being studied.

Powerful lights, used in conjunction with low magnification, wide aperture binoculars, enable a skilled observer to identify many bats in flight and facilitates estimates of feeding densities. Infra-red lights, combined with image intensifiers (which amplify available light) are better, because they do not disturb bats, but this equipment is expensive, and detail and colour are lost. Image intensifiers are particularly useful for watching roosts, especially those containing species which emerge after dark.

'Bat detectors' are devices which have a microphone to detect the ultrasonic cries of bats and in their simplest form, convert the signals into frequencies audible to the range of human hearing. Some bats produce high intensity sounds which can be heard hundreds of metres away, while others make very little noise, and for detection need to be within about two metres of the microphone. With good equipment and a lot of skill, most bat species can be identified.

The ability to identify individuals is important in many studies. Generally bats do not show characters which can allow remote identification, although sometimes individuals with albinism or torn wings can be individally recognised. Various temporary marking methods are available as well as permanent rings. Bats fitted with small radio transmitters and tiny lights, have yielded immensely valuable results, which could not have been obtained in any other way. All these techniques can cause damage to bats and their populations, therefore great care is needed in all research projects to ensure the bats do not suffer.

2
Conservation Problems and Achievements

The species composition and abundance of bats will have varied enormously in the past, due to changing climate and vegetative cover. These factors are still operating, but human activities are now a greater influence on bats.

Compared with birds, bats have received little attention from naturalists and hence our knowledge of the distribution of Europe's 30 species of bat is relatively poor. Even worse is our perception of the abundance of each species. Also, there is little documentation of the size of historic populations and so our appreciation of changes has come mostly from recent observations.

POPULATION CHANGES

Prehistoric Populations

Perhaps the most significant environmental change is the loss of forests and as a result, *Myotis bechsteinii* seems to have suffered more than other species. In several archaeological excavations, bat bones dated at about 3,000 years old have included a high proportion of *M. bechsteinii*, often in areas where the species has not been found in historic times. Other species such as *Plecotus austriacus* in Britain, used to occur about 300 kilometres further north than its present range.

Recent Populations

Despite the lack of much historic documentation, gradually a picture is developing of the former abundance of bats. Often this relies on anecdotal comments by old people, combined with observations of sites where estimates of former colony size can be made. Various clues can be used to indicate earlier occupation by bats, including piles of guano and stained or worn rock. Caves in soft limestone can have cavities worn in the roof by claws of bats grasping the rock over a long period of time.

But what evidence is there that bats have suffered declines and, more particularly, what were the causes?

If losses were due only to 'natural' events and were not a result of human activity, then there would be no need, or even ability to change the course of events. However, if declines were caused by us, stopping or reversing them may be possible if appropriate action is taken. Throughout most of Europe there are roost sites which have been traditionally used, perhaps for centuries, where bats are no longer found.

Caves which once sheltered colonies of hundreds or thousands of bats now have none. In western France a 7,000 strong colony of *Miniopterus schreibersii* disappeared in a decade from the 1950s. Similarly, in one limestone cave in Romania, numbers of *M. schreibersii* fell from about 2,500 bats in 1974 to 150 in 1979. In the same period *Myotis blythi* declined from about 4,500 to 175 and *Rhinolophus mehelyi* from 500 to 125. It is believed these colonies, were considerably larger in the 1950s, but accurate estimates had not been made.

Also in the 1950s and 1960s, colonies of *Myotis myotis* were disappearing throughout Europe. A colony of 3,000 in a Polish church disappeared, as well as other colonies in the Ardennes of Belgium and Luxembourg.

In the stone mines near Maastricht, Netherlands, which are of immense historic importance to Europe as a whole, and which are being destroyed by quarrying for a local cement factory, *Myotis dasycneme* was once commonly found in winter, but since most of the breeding colonies in southern Netherlands are gone, few remain to hibernate in the tunnels.

Throughout Belgium, Federal Republic of Germany, Democratic Republic of Germany, Switzerland and Poland, populations of the delicate *Rhinolophus hipposideros* rapidly declined in the 1950s and 1960s and now the species is virtually extinct in large areas of north west Europe. In the central and north western areas of

Bohemia in Czechoslovakia, the species is now very rare, but in the upland areas of the Sudeten Highlands, bordering Poland, the declines are generally about 10-50 per cent. Several well established colonies in Yugoslavia have also disappeared in the last 25 years. In Britain, it is now extinct in parts of its former range where it was common early this century.

In southern Britain the much larger *Rhinolophus ferrumequinum* is estimated to have numbered 300,000 bats at the beginning of this century, but now only 3,000 remain. Much of this decline occurred between 1950 and 1980, with individual colonies, estimated at many thousands, virtually dying out. There were once at least 58 nursery colonies, but now ten or more babies are born each year only, in twelve colonies. Other former breeding sites are still being discovered even though no bats remain.

Substantial reductions in abundance are not confined to the rarer species. The most common species in Britain is *Pipistrellus pipistrellus*, which largely depends on houses for its nurseries. It declined by 62 per cent from 1978 to 1986. Nothing is known about changes occurring before 1978, but although colonies numbering over 1,000 bats were not unusual 30 years ago, only a few approaching that size are known today.

The examples given so far are mostly in central and northern Europe, but similar declines have been recorded in the southern countries.

Generally, there are few documented records of colony decline, in areas bordering the Mediterranean. Nevertheless, local people are aware of the disappearance of bats and can sometimes identify the cause.

Overall, most of the records concerning declines are related to species which breed or hibernate in caves, often in large conspicuous colonies. Only eleven of Europe's 30 species can be described as being originally more or less dependent on caves for breeding and hibernation. Nowadays 16 have substantial populations using caves for hibernation and another five species occasionally winter in them. The latter group (*Barbastella barbastellus*, *Plecotus* spp., *Pipistrellus pipistrellus* and *Myotis bechsteinii*), are species which may form large aggregations in some areas, for instance, *B. barbastellus* in Poland and Czechoslovakia and *P. pipistrellus* in Romania, but generally they are only sporadically found underground.

Other species are termed 'tree bats', implying they originally lived most of the time in tree hollows. Finding these bats takes much more effort and hence documented observations are few. Indeed, there is a great tendency for these 'tree bats' to be highly nomadic moving frequently, sometimes many kilometres between roosts, so making consistent observations difficult.

Our perception of which species have declined and which show the greatest loss is also coloured by the ease with which they are seen. Anecdotal information suggests the 'tree species' may have suffered badly, especially in countries with a high level of agricultural development and low in forest cover such as Denmark and Britain. In the past *Nyctalus noctula* was often seen flying in large numbers at sunset, (exploiting the cockchafer beetles, *Melolontha* spp), and it was not unusual to count 50 to 200 bats feeding over a small field. In lowland agricultural areas the species is now virtually absent and remaining populations are associated with habitats having a large proportion of trees and pasture. It appears to have survived relatively better in urban areas where parkland and other areas of grassland are common.

Apart from *N. noctula*, several 'tree species' have adapted to be more or less dependent on buildings (for example *N. leisleri* and *P. pipistrellus*). Despite this close proximity to people, these bats are often not noticed and few observations have been made.

Although almost all long term changes in bats have been regressive, one species has shown increases. *Myotis daubentonii* has increased in two sites in Britain and in a few areas of the Netherlands, Federal Republic of Germany, Denmark and Czechoslovakia. However, it is uncertain whether this is a real increase in density, or whether the destruction of roosts is restricting bats to the remaining sites where they can be counted.

To summarise, there is a lot of information scattered throughout Europe suggesting some bat populations have declined substantially this century and local extinctions have already occurred.

CAUSES OF DECLINE AND CONTINUING THREATS

European bats have two basic needs; firstly places to roost and secondly insect food. Anything which affects the number and variety of either of these will inevitably affect bats.

Climate

European bats are mostly small animals (body mass range 4 - 40 grammes), which are dependent on suitable roost temperatures if they are to survive. They can influence their local temperature by forming appropriately sized clusters which enable each bat to contribute a small amount of heat to the group. Reduction in cluster size or lowering of the roost temperature may reduce the value of a site, resulting in bats moving away if they are to survive. This kind of problem is believed to have been one of the contributory causes for the decline of *R. hipposideros* in central and northern Europe. The mean annual temperature has dropped slightly in those areas, causing the cave temperatures to fall, and this is one possible reason for the loss of nurseries in the Polish uplands around Czestochowa - Krakow. However, there are many other possible causes which could be due directly or indirectly to human influences.

It is well known that bad weather can cause high mortality at any time of the year. In winter bats found dead with no remaining food reserves tend to be juveniles but all age classes can be affected. Severe prolonged cold weather, with a high wind-chill factor, causes bats to utilise extra energy to resist freezing or to arouse and fly to warmer places in which to continue hibernation. Early in 1986, when Finland and the eastern Baltic S.S.R's experienced temperatures of -40 degrees Celsius with strong east winds, bats were seen flying west. Many were picked up in Belgium and the Netherlands, including ringed bats from eastern areas.

In summer, around parturition and during lactation, energy demands are greatest for the females. Periods of cold wet weather reduce the availability of flying insects, and this lack of food can cause bats to abandon their young. Occasionally this occurs to whole colonies and with no new recruitment to the population, declines of up to 40 per cent in one year have been recorded. This kind of loss was also recorded for 32 colonies of *P. pipistrellus* in 1978 in Britain. Juvenile mortality is often less than five per cent in good years, so populations may recover quickly.

Landscape

Forestry

Alteration of habitats results in changes to the composition of bat communities. Three thousand years ago much of the lowland of central and northern Europe was under a forest regime, with the trees being mostly broad-leaved species. The highlands were dominated by conifers. Through the neolithic and bronze ages and especially in the later iron age, the forests were felled, partly to make way for agriculture, and also as a source of charcoal for artisans who made and fashioned iron. Clearly, those bat species which depended on large tracts of mature forests were likely to decline, while those preferring open range habitats or forest edge, were likely to benefit in the developing patchwork of woodlands.

Present forest policies in many countries favour planting large areas of monoculture, usually conifers. Moreover these are often alien species which lack the large numbers of insect types commonly associated with native species. Also, these extensive tracts of monocultures, especially if planted in previously unforested areas, tend to suffer from outbreaks of insect pests such as pine beauty moth, *Panolis flammea*, or pine looper, *Bupalus piniaria*.

Often, drastic action is taken, involving aerial spraying with pesticides to control these pests. Bats in these areas accumulate the chemicals by eating other treated insects and some die. Most spraying is done when bats are giving birth or raising their young, and non-lethal concentrations may impair breeding success, as the pesticide passes to the offspring through the mother's milk.

Most intensive forestry involves removal of damaged, moribund or dead trees, to help prevent the spread of fungal diseases to healthy trees. However, moribund trees often have holes which provide roosts, and a succession of insect food for bats. In parts of Europe such as southern Federal Republic of Germany, forestry practice involves removal of selected trees from amongst other mature trees allowing natural regeneration in the clearings. By not creating large areas of clearfell, the forest communities of animals and plants are almost in an equilibrium.

Overall, European countries average 33.5 per cent forest cover, with Eire, Netherlands and Britain each having less than ten per cent. In parts of Britain, up to 30 per cent of broad-leaved woodland has been felled since 1945, and replaced mostly with cereal crops.

Agriculture

Historically, as forests were cleared, some areas were used for arable crops and some for pasture. The details vary as to how these changes took place in different parts of Europe, but the essential processes were similar. In some of the poorer areas, agricultural methods have barely changed for hundreds of years, but over most of Europe the change has been rapid and generally harmful to bats. An average of 28 per cent of the land per country is now arable, with Norway, Sweden and Finland each having less than ten per cent. Removing forests to make farm land reduces insect populations and tree hole roost sites.

Perhaps the most important agricultural change to affect bats, is the reduction in area of pasture and increase in size of fields. Permanent, unimproved grassland has a rich diversity of plant and insect life. Some insects emerge only over a few days each year, while others are available to bats for several months. Not only is the variety and abundance of insects important, but so are sheltered places where bats may feed on them. Consequently, a patchwork of fields, copses, woods and hedgerows provides ideal habitat.

Old pastures which have been ploughed and reseeded with a few highly productive species of grass, only support a few species of insect.

Farmers are increasingly keeping cattle inside buildings; a practice which has many economic advantages. Fewer people are needed to look after the animals whose conversion rates are greatly improved by living in a warm environment. The old practice of putting livestock in fields resulted in some of the grass being damaged by trampling, as well as finance being required for installing and maintaining stock-proof fences. However, cattle dung accumulates in the stock yard and may be spread on fields only once or twice each year, or sold for other uses such as mushroom growing compost. The former practice of putting cattle on pasture at regular intervals throughout the year, allowed the production of several generations of dung insects. Many of these insects, for example the beetles *Aphodius* spp. and *Geotrupes* spp., are very important to bats, especially at lactation or just prior to hibernation.

Plate 4. Cockchafer beetles, Melolontha spp., have almost disappeared over much of northern Europe due mostly to loss of pasture. This decline of big bats can probably be partially linked to this loss (photo: R. E. Stebbings).

A relatively new problem occurs when drugs are given to livestock. Systemic treatment of cattle with Ivermetin, to control internal parasites, results in the chemical being excreted in the dung. Dung from these animals poison insects which normally exploit that food resource. This problem relates equally to animals kept in buildings as well as those living in fields.

Artificial fertilisers are used to improve the productivity of permanent pastures. These chemicals gradually kill sensitive plant species by changing soil pH, or by more vigorous plants shading them out, which further reduces insect diversity. Sometimes insects such as craneflies, *Tipula* spp, reach high densities and damage pasture. Pesticide is then applied and apart from reducing the numbers of insects available for bats, poisoning of bats by the pesticide may occur.

Many insect species time their life cycle to pupate when the plants begin to dry as they flower. When pasture is cut too early, as in the recent practice of cutting for silage, the variety of insects is affected.

Removal of boundaries to make larger fields, not only reduces insects through loss of vegetation, but, where hedgerows are involved also removes shelter and roosts in hollow trees. This problem is greatest in Britain where 182,000 kilometres of hedgerows have been removed since 1945. Modern ploughing which is often deeper and closer to field boundaries, removes natural vegetation and damages the surface feeding roots of trees. Such trees may be killed or become more vulnerable to being blown down in gales. Surface mean wind speeds are increased following the removal of woodland and hedgerow shelter, thus making it more difficult for insects to fly on windy nights and therefore reducing the amount of food available for bats. Also this increased exposure of remaining trees will increase the wind-chill factor in winter, so reducing the suitability of remaining hollow trees to be used for hibernation.

Rivers, Lakes and Riparian Habitats

Marshland, flood plains and riparian woodland are amongst the most productive areas for insects and most bats exploit them extensively.

However, these areas have long been recognised by farmers for their productivity, and drainage operations have been pursued for hundreds of years. With modern equipment almost any marshland can be drained and turned over to agriculture.

By cutting artificial dykes and canals across wetlands, water tables are reduced and since water flows rapidly to the sea through canalised rivers, less water soaks down to replenish aquifers. Canalisation of rivers has the same affect and usually involves removal of riverside vegetation and trees to enable large dredging machines to work unobstructed.

These activities all serve to reduce insect abundance and variety, as well as hollow tree roosts. Even canalisation of rivers eliminates many insect species with aquatic larval stages because the increased speed of water flow is unsuitable. Several species of bat feed low over water (*M. dasycneme, M. daubentonii, B.*

barbastellus and *P. pipistrellus*), and slow flowing, sheltered water with overhanging trees, provides optimum conditions. Many insects, such as mayflies, *Ephemeroptera*, caddis, *Trichoptera* and Chironomidae, are caught as they float up to the water surface and take off.

Golf Courses and Parks

These kinds of places tend to be excellent for bats, because there are lots of old trees which have hollows for roosting, large areas of grassland for insects and sheltered areas where insects can fly and be caught for food. Unfortunately, hollow branches are cut off, as they are thought to present a hazard. Grass is sprayed with pesticides, particularly the organochlorine chemical, Chlordane to kill worms because their 'casts' interfere with golf balls and lawn mowers. Bats are known to have died by accumulating this pesticide, presumably because they have fed on insects emerging from treated grassland.

Some trees with hollows which are considered safe, have the holes filled with cement to help reduce the rate of decay inside the tree, but this excludes bats and other animals.

Urban Areas

These are generally good for bats for the quantity of both insects and the number of roosts found there, especially when gardens have mature trees. Also they are relatively safe, sheltered places for bats to live providing their roosts are not harmed.

Buildings

Bats use all kinds of buildings, both the rooms and spaces created for human living areas, as well as gaps created at the time of building, or formed inadvertently as the structure deteriorated.

Most buildings in Europe are less than 100 years old and very few are older then 1,000 years. However, buildings now constitute one of the most important roost resources for the majority of bats and all species have been found in them. Indeed provision of permanent buildings beyond the tree line in Norway, Sweden and Finland has allowed bats to exploit the abundant food in the short summer of those sub-arctic areas.

Most of the problems encountered by bats in buildings are a result of renovation or demolition work. Bats are entombed or excluded when stone or brickwork is repointed. Most old castles or churches have loose rubble-filled walls or columns, in which large numbers of bats will hibernate if access between the facing stones can be gained. Old bridges, aqueducts, walls, and buttresses are all used by substantial numbers of bats both as nursery sites and for hibernation. Renovation of these buildings involving rebuilding or the filling in of cavities and cracks, deprives bats of roosts. The importance of 'solid' walls to bats is greatly underestimated since bats are usually only found when a wall is pulled down. However, a thirteenth century, derelict castle in Wales, was to be repaired by repointing three metre thick walls to make them safe. Previous studies had shown up to 40 *R. ferrumequinum* used two small cavities in these walls, but subsequent observations revealed at least 300 bats of four species with nursery colonies, while smaller numbers of other species were thought to live in crevices. Now repairs are carefully planned to ensure these major roosts remain undisturbed.

Another example of the importance of cavities in stone walls comes from a survey of stone built bridges in north Yorkshire, England. Of 185 bridges examined, 58 (31 per cent) had significant numbers of bats using them. There were hibernating and nursery colonies, with one bridge having three species, totalling at least 150 bats at one time, (*M. daubentonii, M. nattereri*, and *N. noctula*).

A growing practice is to smother bridges in liquid concrete, which is blown under high pressure at the stone surface. The intention is to fill all the cracks and crevices in one operation, to avoid elaborate and expensive scaffolding required to repoint each crack by hand. Clearly this procedure is extremely damaging to bats and large numbers must be killed as a result.

Old farm buildings with roughly built walls, often have poor foundations. Cracks in the walls allow bats to crawl inside. These buildings are generally too small for modern farming equipment and they are usually removed and replaced with large, thin-walled structures, having no suitable roosting potential.

Bats have been excluded or killed in some old buildings in Italy, where, at the bats entrance urine and droppings were said to have corroded walls built of limestone.

Bats have been excluded from old buildings such as churches and castles, where in the past they could fly directly inside but where now windows have been installed.

Older houses frequently had wine, food or fuel cellars with an entrance leading directly to the outside. Bats used them mostly for hibernation although some were used as nurseries. Cellars have often been filled in or have had access holes blocked, mainly for security reasons. Likewise, country houses tended to have permanently open fuel or tool store-rooms which allowed bats free access, but again, for security reasons, present day owners fit doors and keep them closed. 'Tidying up' operations in and around buildings often serve to exclude bats, especially the Rhinolophidae, which prefer to fly directly to their roosting position.

Buildings containing valuables increasingly are being fitted with electronic security devices. Older buildings especially, frequently have bat colonies and gaps around windows or wood panelling which allow bats access to rooms and set off alarms. The solution is sometimes seen to be the elimination of bats, whereas blocking holes or changing the position or type of sensors would be sufficient.

In more modern buildings, especially in northern Europe, cavity walls are filled with insulation material. These cavities are known to contain many bat species both in summer and winter. Undoubtedly, bats will have been entombed and killed by the process and others excluded.

A major cause of bat deaths is remedial timber treatments in buildings. A large number of chemicals are sprayed in buildings to kill wood-boring beetles or to control wood-rotting fungi. Many of these chemicals are lethal to bats, especially when they are in high vapour concentrations for a few weeks after spraying. A few chemicals are very persistent and will continue to kill or harm bats for many years after treatment. Amongst the most lethal and persistent chemicals are the organochlorine pesticides, especially Dieldrin and Pentachlorophenol, but the most commonly used chemical, Lindane (gamma HCH), has killed enormous numbers of bats. Bats have small bodies with relatively large surface areas through which the chemicals readily pass. Consequently these animals are particularly susceptible to these treatments. Also they frequently roost in close contact with treated surfaces, with their nostrils usually in the boundary air layer which contains high vapour concentrations. Bats spend much of the time grooming their fur and membranes and hence they ingest dust and crystalline deposits from the timber. Although high levels of pesticide kill bats, the effects of sub-lethal concentrations are unknown, but may contribute, with other problems or disease to reduce survival.

While building styles in the past created all kinds of places which bats utilise, modern architecture is limiting the range of species which might live in buildings. With integral insulation and prefabricated panels, which is a common technique in many central, northern and north eastern countries, bats will not find access or suitable roost sites.

Old, disused tunnels of all kinds (road, railway and canal), especially those which are brick or stone lined, are often important places for bats throughout the year. These tunnels tend to have large cavities behind the lining and because most bats are secretive, they are not often visible.

Tunnels used by solid-fuelled or diesel engined transport, have soot or other mineral deposits on their surface. It takes up to 50 years for salts to fall off sufficiently to allow bats to use the site. Many tunnels already used by bats have been lost to them, as entrances considered dangerous have been blocked, or the tunnels are used for other activities from rifle shooting to storage depots, and even municipal nuclear fallout shelters.

Other kinds of tunnel, especially old military defence systems, have often developed a significant use by bats, but then have been lost when they are blocked or used to dump toxic or nuclear waste. In western Poland, the proposal to use some of the former defence tunnels in the Lubuskie Lake District as a repository for nuclear waste, threatens the most important bat hibernation site (Nietoperek Bat Reserve) in northern Europe.

Caves and Mines

These provide the environment many bats seek. Species such as *Rhinolophus, Miniopterus* and some *Myotis* (for example *M. myotis* and *M. blythi*) are mostly cave-dwelling animals throughout the year and are frequently found in colonies of hundreds or thousands.

Caves are patchily distributed and geologically are mostly associated with limestone outcrops. The largest concentrations of caves are in the countries bordering the Mediterranean, such as Greece, Yugoslavia, Italy and Spain. In Slovenia (northern Yugoslavia) more than 5,000 caves are already known, from an area of about 7,000 square kilometres, with the total number expected to be more than 10,000. In most caves only a few bats may be found, but some caves are immensely important because thousands of bats from a wide area gather in them. Unfortunately, the largest numbers of bats tend to be found in the largest caves which are either visited by speleologists, or opened for general tourism. Solid walls have been built across entrances, blocking access for bats, or lights installed which disturb and drive them away. The fate of these evicted animals is unknown, but because bats had been using these optimum sites for hundreds or thousands of years, they may have difficulty finding other such suitable roosts. Disturbance of an increasingly large number of caves, with the development of sport caving and tourism, is likely to be a major factor in the decline of some bats.

Caves and mines are often convenient 'holes in the ground', in which rubbish is deposited and this has been the cause of the loss of a large number of important bat roosts in almost every country. With local authorities becoming more safety conscious, dangerous caves and especially mines have been blocked, with no account being taken of the bats and other wildlife which might be using them. Many colonies have been lost in this way. In Britain there are about 250,000 coal mine shafts or tunnels and a similar number of old metalliferous mines. Large schemes are in operation to seal the shafts, mostly employing solid caps.

Speleologists have also damaged roosts in three additional ways, apart from the disturbance they cause. Firstly, when caves were gated by caving clubs, usually their concern was to prevent vandalism to rock formations. Because many entrances are in remote places, solid steel plates were installed, and this not only prevented access by bats, but by restricting convection air currents, changed the cave temperature, making it unsuitable for bats. Secondly, acetylene, or other gas lamps are used, which produce harmful gases and the spent calcium carbide from the acetylene lamps is often dropped in the cave together with food and other rubbish, so causing pollution. Thirdly, many caving groups try to extend the known cave, by blasting rock with explosives, which is known to have killed bats both from the shock wave and from residual gasses.

Archaeologists have caused extensive disturbance in caves, driving out bats when 'digs' last for several weeks.

Occasionally, quarrying has revealed hidden caves or mines which subsequently became significant bat roosts, but later some were lost by continuing quarry operations.

Cliffs and Quarries

Climbers cause disturbance and damage to bats but the extent of the problem is unknown. Very large numbers of bats are known to roost and hibernate in cliff crevices, and these can be disturbed and sometimes killed when pitons, to secure climbers ropes, are driven into rock faces. This problem is known to be affecting *N. noctula* in Switzerland, but a similar problem is probably occurring in many countries. Bats have often been found when a fissured quarry face is brought down through quarrying operations, and in some sites bat nurseries as well as hibernacula are involved. Because a quarry may be the only bare and fissured rock face in a large area, bats which like to roost in such places, inevitably will congregate there. *Nyctalus, Pipistrellus, Eptesicus, Barbastellus, Plecotus*, with some *Myotis* species and *Tadarida*, are all known to use these kinds of crevices.

Predation and Disease

Little is known about the 'natural' causes of death in bats. A number of disease organisms have been identified in dead bats which may have been the cause of death. However, since 1985 it has been recognised that a rabies-like virus is present in some populations of European bats, making necessary a careful evaluation of the risk this poses to people and wildlife. The virus has been found in moribund or freshly dead bats as far apart as Denmark, Poland and Spain. Although mostly found in one of the largest bats, *Eptesicus serotinus*, it does occur in other species. Observations suggest the virus may not occur in other animals, but further experimentation and a detailed appraisal continues. Perhaps most important is the fact that the virus is likely to have been present for very many years without causing problems to bat workers, other naturalists, the public or other animals, domestic or wild.

Nevertheless, it is vital for people to take care when handling bats. As with other wildlife, especially animals which are grounded and probably sick, it is important to avoid being bitten. If someone is bitten by a bat, the wound should be cleaned immediately with soap, and medical advice sought. Fresh dead bats should be sent to a virus testing laboratory for examination. Providing this precaution is taken, there seems to be no justification in excluding or removing colonies, even where a virus positive bat has been identified.

It is not yet known how significant the disease is in reducing bat populations, but these aspects are now under study.

Predation is mostly a casual happening by a variety of opportunists, from owls and woodpeckers to squirrels, rats and weasels. Domestic and feral cats appear to catch large numbers of bats, which sometimes has a significant affect on a local population. Particular damage is done when cats catch bats flying through narrow cave entrances. One cat was known to eat 22 bats of three species in a few hours, (*R. ferrumequinum, R. hipposideros* and *P. auritus*). These luckless animals were all regurgitated, and it is not known whether the cat killed and ate others. Another cat, sitting on a tree branch hanging low over a canal, caught and killed over 70 *M. daubentonii*, within a few weeks. Approximately one third of 450 bats found dead in Britain in seven years were animals caught by cats. It is not known, however, whether some of those bats may already have been sick and grounded.

Pollution

Bats and their insect food source have been affected by different kinds of pollution and many problems continue. As relatively little sampling has been carried out, the extent of the problem is unknown.

Large areas of central and northern Europe, especially parts of the Federal Republic of Germany, Democratic Republic of Germany, Czechoslovakia, Poland and Sweden, are suffering from 'acid rain', causing the death of vegetation and animals in water courses. Some insects may benefit from the increase in dead timber, but overall the affects on insects and ultimately bats, may be severe. In almost every country, some rivers are seriously polluted from industrial wastes, fertilisers, herbicides, pesticides and farm slurry. Cattle slurry and silage are respectively about 100 and 200 times more polluting than sewage. In Britain in 1985, more than 3,500 cases of river pollution were identified from these sources, and probably others went undetected. This kind of pollution kills many of the water-dependent insects which in turn affects bats, mostly *M. dasycneme* and *M. daubentonii*. Some kinds of pollutants, such as pesticides, may accumulate in insects in sub-lethal concentrations, and they can be concentrated to lethal levels in bats which feed upon them.

*Plate 5. Brown long-eared bats, **Plecotus auritus**, killed by the pesticide, Lindane (gamma HCH), used in a remedial timber treatment in a domestic house (photo: R. E. Stebbings).*

Pesticides used in forestry and agriculture are known to kill bats. In Greece, olive plantations are sprayed by aircraft to control pests and bats have declined in those areas. In some countries high concentrations of DDT and its metabolites, as well as Chlordane and Dieldrin are present in some bats found dead. No systematic surveys nor adequate experiments have been conducted, to assess the affects of sub-lethal levels of various chemicals

Disturbance

If bats are disturbed deliberately or accidentally, they will ultilise energy reserves which they need if they are to survive until spring. One enforced arousal may use up to 40 days worth of reserves, and several such disturbances in one winter may cause bats to starve to death. Disturbance by tourists and naturalists is thought to have resulted in large declines of some populations.

Research

In the 1950s to early 1970s, collecting and field activities of research scientists, and to a lesser extent naturalists, were major causes of local bat declines and extinctions. The problem has been reduced in recent years mostly by education and exchange of information and experiences.

In the past, large numbers of bats, mainly *M. myotis* and *R. ferrumequinum*, were taken for laboratory study and museum collections. Nowadays, small numbers are generally taken, but in some areas no such removal is justified.

One of the earliest endeavours of bat researchers was to find whether bats returned to the same hibernacula each winter and how far bats could 'home' after release some distance from the place of capture. This involved marking bats with numbered metal rings. Large scale forearm ringing began in Germany in the early 1930s with many thousands of bats being marked. A little later similar work began in other areas, notably in the Netherlands. Colonies and populations declined and rapidly disappeared and many bats were found with severe injuries caused by the rings. Ringing usually involved frequent and large-scale disturbance of bats. Some of the cave bat ringing studies involved bringing bats to a central point for processing. Because the bats were in captivity sometimes for hours, they lost a lot of energy which may have reduced survival. Also, other bats may have been frightened away, never to return to the same cave.

It is unclear whether it was the ring injuries or disturbance which caused most mortality. Certainly some populations crashed, to recover only when high level disturbance and ringing ceased. Rings made of hard, smooth, lightweight metal are now used in some countries, which, if correctly applied, cause no damage. However, poor quality rings are still being applied, with inevitable damage to bats.

Natural Disasters and Vandalism

Bats are most vulnerable when living in large aggregations. Single events can effectively eliminate bats from a wide area, especially when nursery colonies are killed. Entire regional populations may have gathered in one site to give birth and raise their young. Colonies in trees may be struck by lightning, or the tree may be blown down. Colonies in caves may be killed by flash floods or blocked entrances.

Similar catastrophes have been the result of deliberate acts of vandalism. Throughout Europe, large numbers of colonies have been destroyed by people. Mostly these have been in buildings and often insecticide smoke generators were used to kill them.

In 1971, 2,000 *P. pipistrellus* were killed by this method in a house near Dumfries, Scotland, while in 1981, 96 hibernating *Myotis* bats were killed in eastern England, by being shot with air gun pellets or set on fire. When explosive fireworks were thrown into a cluster of hibernating *R. ferrumequinum* in south west England in 1978, 35 bats were killed.

Bats being knocked to the ground and killed has been a widespread problem, but perhaps worst of all is the burning of plastic fertilizer bags in caves, the poisonous gases from which, quickly kill bats in residence. Similarly in Greece, bats in caves are killed by fumigation either 'for fun', or because local people are frightened of bats.

We have no way of knowing how many bats have been killed by these kinds of acts, but significant numbers must be involved. Bat declines in some areas can probably be attributed to these kinds of anti-bat activity.

LEGISLATION

International

Two of the instruments of international wildlife law to which various European states have acceded seek both to highlight the conservation problems of bats and to provide protection for them. These are known as the 'Bern' and 'Bonn' Conventions.

1) The Convention on the Conservation of European Wildlife and Natural Habitats ('Bern Convention'. Entered into force 1 June 1982.)

In relation to bats, this convention serves to conserve all species and their natural habitats and to promote co-operation between member states. It was considered particularly important to protect endangered and vulnerable species such as bats, especially as they can be migratory.

Within the convention, *P. pipistrellus* was regarded as a 'protected species' in Appendix III, but all other species were listed in Apendix II, as 'strictly protected animals'.

BERN CONVENTION

Figure 1. States which have ratified the Bern Convention are shown in black and those which are signatories are indicated with hatching.

The strength of this convention lies in the fact that it requires all states who are signatories to undertake specified conservation activities and to enact appropriate legislation before ratification.

In fact, none of those party states who have ratified have enacted adequate legislation to fulfil their obligations under the Convention.

Bern Convention

(Only the European member States as at December 1987 are listed.)

Countries which have ratified: Austria, Denmark, Eire, Finland, Federal Republic of Germany, Greece, Italy, Liechtenstein, Luxembourg, Netherlands, Norway, Portugal, Spain, Sweden, Switzerland and United Kingdom.

Countries which have signed: Belgium and France.

---

2) The Convention on the Conservation of Migratory Species of Wild Animals ('Bonn Convention' 1979.   Entered into force 1 November 1983.)

This convention arose because it was realised that failure to protect a migratory species, at all stages of its migration, could limit the possibilities of its recovery from a population decline. There are two Appendices with all bats in Europe belonging to the Rhinolophidae and Vespertilionidae being in Appendix II.

An oversight caused one of Europe's migratory species, *Tadarida teniotis*, belonging to the family Molossidae, to be omitted. However, this error is being corrected in the first AGREEMENT which is being drafted, and which specifically concerns bats. This draft 'AGREEMENT on the conservation of Bats in Europe' includes all the Microchiroptera.

Unlike the Bern Convention, the Bonn Convention seeks to persuade 'Range States' who have ratified the convention, to make 'arrangements' for the conservation of protected species. It does

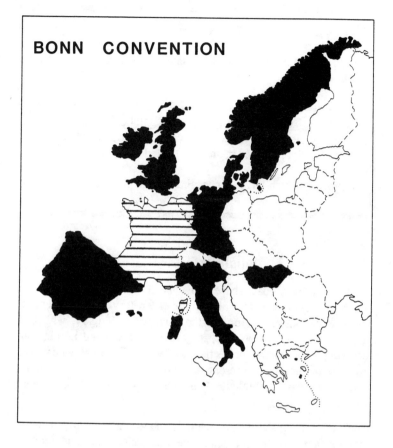

Figure 2. States which have ratified the Bonn Convention are shown in black and those which are signatories are indicated with hatching.

not 'oblige' States to undertake specific actions, but rather suggests what kind of actions ought to be included in 'AGREE-MENTS' to ensure adequate measures are taken for the protection and conservation of protected species.

In order for this convention to become effective in Europe, more Range States are required to accede especially in the east, as bats tend to be more migratory in those areas where the winters are severe.

Bonn Convention

(Only the European member States as at December 1987 are listed.)

Countries which have ratified: Denmark, European Economic Community, Federal Republic of Germany, Hungary, Eire, Italy, Luxembourg, Netherlands, Norway, Portugal, Spain, Sweden and the United Kingdom.

Countries which have signed: France and Greece.

National/State Legislation

Laws to protect bats have now been passed in almost all countries, covering nearly all European territory. Indeed, legislation was passed at the turn of the century in Hungary, with bats in Austria, Finland, Germany, Italy, Liechtenstein and Portugal all receiving some sort of protection by 1940. The areas where bats have no protection at present are, the Isle of Man, Channel Islands, Brussels, Gibraltar, Malta and possibly Albania and Romania.

Much of the legislation however, is inadequate, usually because only the animals are protected and not their roosts and feeding habitat. Also, in spite of legislation having been in force in some places for 50 years or more, there has been no enforcement. Often people in appropriate government agencies are unaware bats are protected (and sometimes when they do know, they do not implement the law).

In some states, conservation forms part of the Forestry Service remit, while in others it falls to the Agriculture Department. But both types of organisation are more involved in the direct economy of their respective countries, so conservation activities are seen as a drain on funds. Hence, only small amounts of money are made available for conservation, whether for protection or management of sites, or for education. Also, there is usually no control or restrictions over research activities, which in some cases may be harmful to bat populations. If bats are considered to be a nuisance, they may be killed by the local authorities, even though they are known to be protected. This is often done as a result of ignorance about the life history of bats and of ways to solve problems.

A good example of the value of passing protective legislation was shown in Britain. Prior to 1975, neither bats nor their roosts were protected. At that time, approximately 25 people were interested in bats but only two or three spent more than about five days per year studying them. For 20 years previously, a few enthusiasts had tried to stimulate others to become more active, but with little success. Then in 1975, the Wild Creatures and Wild Plants Act was passed, which protected only the two endangered species, *Rhinolophus ferrumequinum* and *Myotis myotis*. It became illegal to catch (to take or remove from the wild) any of these bats unless a licence to do so had been issued by the Nature Conservancy Council, the governmental agency charged with the task of implementation of the legislation. Despite a considerable amount of publicity there was almost no increase in bat interest either while the bill passed through its various stages in Parliament or subsequently with the issue of booklets and other education materials. However, following the passing of the Wildlife and Countryside Act, 1981, which protected all bats and their roosts, a tidal wave of interest surged across the country, mainly of ordinary people, who cared for the environment and especially wished to help these much maligned animals. The interest could only have been generated as the result of the huge amount of publicity in the media, combined with vigorous education campaigns. Within two years over 40 local bat groups were established, linked by a national co-ordinating panel whose secretariat was based at the Flora and Fauna Preservation Society, London. Therefore it was the legislation which triggered this vitally important development in the conservation of bats in Britain.

Education

Few states have made substantial efforts to inform the public about bats, their protection and the need to conserve populations. Often, most publicity has been provided by biologists studying bats in universities and museums, and even by amateur naturalists. However, a number of countries now have education programmes tied to a conservation programme of survey and protection. Most notable is the substantial amount of excellent educational material published in Switzerland, but a number of countries have booklets and posters, particularly Netherlands, Denmark, Finland, France, parts of the Federal Republic of Germany and Britain. Education programmes are also under way in Belgium, Spain, Czechoslovakia and Estonia SSR.

In Denmark, following the discovery in 1985 of the rabies-related virus in *E. serotinus*, there have been many radio and television programmes together with articles in the press, explaining to the public about the life-style of bats. To the surprise of the bat biologists, most people were not particularly concerned about the problem, but instead sought advice on how they should react. Generally householders were persuaded to keep their bats, whilst appreciating that sick bats should not be picked up with the bare hand. Perhaps most extraordinary and gratifying was the fact that people were prepared to get rid of their domestic cats (which are most likely to find and pick up diseased animals) rather than their bats.

Less than half of the European countries have large numbers of amateur bat enthusiasts, but by 1986 in Britain, about 1,500 people belonged to local bat groups. One of the most important roles of these groups is to advise and educate householders who are concerned about bats. They also provide advice to all kinds of service industries which may come across bats, for example builders and firms specialising in timber treatments.

Protection of Sites

Some sites shelter bats which seasonally gather from tens of thousands of square kilometres. This habit makes them very vulnerable, because catastrophes, whether natural or man-made, could eliminate bats from a large area in an instant. Thus, biologists studying such places have regarded them as being in need of protection. However, relatively few bat roosts have received protection. Occasionally parts of caves and buildings developed for tourism, were given sanctuary status. Even so, as the bats in those were frequently deprived of their most important roost areas and confined to less suitable places, their numbers subsequently declined.

Sometimes caves with important bat colonies, have been protected with metal grilles and gates to prevent unauthorised human access. However, on occasions these artificial barriers have caused too much obstruction, either to the air interchange between the cave and the outside, or to the bats, preventing them from freely flying through. As a result, bats stay away. Other grilles have caused bats to abandon caves when built in the wrong place or if they were installed during the wrong season. However, there is now sufficient knowledge to prevent these sorts of problems happening in the future.

Although mostly hibernation places have been protected such as caves, mines and other underground sites, little effort has been devoted to protecting nurseries, either in buildings or trees. But these nurseries are key sites requiring protection, because they contain all the breeding females from a wide area. In several countries, a few have been protected, but usually they were in public buildings such as churches, castles, schools or municipal offices, where protection was relatively easy. Clearly, it is difficult to give statutory protection to colonies in privately owned domestic houses, because inevitably, some restrictions would be needed as to the way the building could be used. Also, there would need to be controls on the methods and timing of building maintenance.

Nevertheless, some efforts are being made to address this problem, and through better education, more property owners are agreeing to measures which will ensure survival of a bat roost. Grants and other incentives can be given in a few circumstances.

In some ways a more difficult problem is the need to protect feeding habitat. Because bats range over large areas when searching for insects, it is necessary to consider the management of areas covering many square kilometres, even for small colonies. A typical feeding density for the small *P. pipistrellus,* in good habitat, is one bat per three hectares, so even for colonies of 100 bats, a total area of three square kilometres might be required. Larger species such as *M. myotis* and *R. ferrumequinum* range at least 15 kilometres radius from their roost each night (700 square kilometres) and if different roost loci are used by one colony during the year, the scale of the problem can be appreciated. However, within these areas there will be zones of differing feeding quality and only the best areas might need protection, but a detailed study would be necessary to identify where the bats spend most of their time.

Bats should be considered as one of the most important faunal elements in the assessment of conservation priorities for habitats.

Conservation Strategies for Endangered Species

Until recently no country had attempted to consider overall strategies for the conservation of rare or endangered species. Generally, if any action was taken, it was limited to protection of sites, usually in 'fire brigade' actions when roosts were threatened with damage or loss. Sometimes such urgent unplanned action, perhaps involving building or grilling operations, has itself inadvertently damaged a roost, causing bats to abandon it. These problems must be avoided and it is vital to develop a coherent action plan to ensure representative elements of the endangered species populations are adequately protected. This will always involve research to establish how many roosts there are, the numbers of bats in each, how they relate to each other, what insects the bats eat and where they feed. From this, key sites can be identified.

No international collaborative projects to protect bats have been attempted and this is why the Bern and Bonn Conventions are so important. These animals, which mostly spend their summers and winters in widely separated and differing kinds of roosts, need unified campaigns across Europe if they are to survive.

STATUS OF EUROPEAN BATS: A SUMMARY

Species	Status
Family Rhinolophidae	
Rhinolophus ferrumequinum (Schreber)	E
Rhinolophus hipposideros (Bechstein)	E
Rhinolophus blasii Peters	E
Rhinolophus euryale Blasius	V
Rhinolophus mehelyi Matschie	R(?E)
Family Vespertilionidae	
Myotis mystacinus (Kuhl)	V
Myotis brandtii (Eversmann)	V
Myotis emarginatus (Geoffroy)	E
Myotis capaccinii (Bonaparte)	V(?E)
Myotis daubentonii (Kuhl)	?Nt
Myotis dasycneme (Boie)	E
Myotis nattereri (Kuhl)	V
Myotis bechsteinii (Kuhl)	R(?E)
Myotis myotis (Borkhausen)	E
Myotis blythi (Tomes)	E
Pipistrellus pipistrellus (Schreber)	V
Pipistrellus nathusii (Keyserling & Blasius)	V
Pipistrellus kuhli (Kuhl)	V
Pipistrellus savii (Bonaparte)	V
Eptesicus serotinus (Schreber)	Nt
Eptesicus nilssonii (Keyserling & Blasius)	Nt
Vespertilio murinus Linnaeus	R
Nyctalus noctula (Schreber)	V
Nyctalus leisleri (Kuhl)	V
Nyctalus lasiopterus (Schreber)	R
Miniopterus schreibersii (Kuhl)	E
Plecotus auritus (Linnaeus)	V
Plecotus austriacus (Fischer)	V
Barbastella barbastellus (Schreber)	V(?E)
Family Molossidae	
Tadarida teniotis (Rafinesque)	V

E = Endangered, V = Vulnerable, R = Rare, Nt = Not threatened.
Note : The status recorded here is for European bats as a whole, but individual countries may have different categories. Even bats marked here as endangered are common in some areas.

3

Conservation Needs

Conservation strategies for bats, both nationally and internationally, are important and need to be carefully considered. Bats do not
recognise state boundaries and frequently they spend different
parts of their life cycle in two or more countries. The aim should
be for each state to develop a strategy in liaison with adjacent
states, so conservation measures in one country will not be wasted
by lack of appropriate action in another. Criteria are needed to
allow judgements of whether particular sites are sufficiently important to be given special protection. Regular reassessment is
needed to accommodate improved knowledge and changes in
status. Because of the variations in status of each species across
Europe, inevitably, a species may be regarded as abundant in one
country and in no particular need of special protection, but, in
another State, could be designated as an endangered species requiring roosts to be nature reserves.

Simple conservation strategies for individual States should be in-
stituted, but allow flexibility as detailed policy is developed. A
framework is needed which appraises such things as: legislation -
- is it adequate; implementation -- how much more could be
done; education -- do people know about bats and the law; research and survey -- what is known about the distribution, status
and needs for each species; threats -- what are they; conservation -- what needs to be done. The rest of this chapter is devoted
to possible solutions to these problems. There is a lot of
knowledge to draw upon in Europe and the Chiroptera Specialist
Group of the SSC will help any State requiring assistance.

LEGISLATION

No European country has passed fully adequate legislation to
ensure the long term survival of bats. Of course, legislation in

itself is not sufficient, but it does show people that bats are threatened and that governments recognise the need to take conservation measures.

Legislation needs to give specific protection to all aspects of a bats life history: the animal, its roosts and feeding habitat. It also needs to provide a framework in which any necessary scientific research is permitted by licences. The exact wording of legislation is vital to the way in which the law may be enforced. For example in Great Britain, by using the words '...if any person intentionally kills...', enforcement is made virtually impossible because it is extremely difficult to prove 'intent' unless the defendant admits to the fact. In English law, the word 'reckless' is better than 'intentional' because a person may have accidentally killed bats without having considered the effect of his actions. People should know the law of their country and should take reasonable precautions to avoid contraventions.

The legislation needs to prevent the killing, injuring or taking of a wild bat, as well as giving protection to roost sites, even if bats are not in residence, and to prevent the disturbance of bats while in roosts. Also, it needs to make illegal the possession of bats (or even parts of), whether alive or dead, as well as their exchange or sale.

However, licenses for specific, well defined and refereed purposes such as research or conservation and education, will need to be issued to appropriate people. A licence would not be required for taking an injured bat, either for killing as an act of humanity, or if the bat was to be tended, with the aim of releasing it to the wild upon recovery.

The bat roosts must be protected at all times, even though some are occupied only seasonally. Thus, caves and all kinds of underground structures should not be filled in, sealed or even grilled without appropriate permission, or a licence being granted. The same must be true for buildings, where there are two main problems: Firstly, repair, maintenance and alterations may destroy or obstruct entrances to roosts. Advice should be sought from the implementation agency on how to minimize damage or disturbance to bats. The use of highly toxic chemicals to treat timbers in roosts, should not be permitted now suitable alternatives are available. Secondly, some people do not like bats in buildings and may not be persuaded to keep them, but provision must be made to allow advice to be given by appropriate experts on how to get rid of bats without harming them. Lack of such a clause in the legislation may cause people to kill bats without notifying the authorities. As with any law, it is important to retain the good will of the people. Legislation has to allow by licensing, the killing of bats if they are shown to be causing actual damage to people or property, if no other solution is practical. (Such occurrences are very rare.)

Implementation of Legislation

There is no value in passing legislation unless there is a statutory organisation vested with the authority to implement the laws and administer its requirements. The authority needs an adequate budget for administrative and field staff, for research, reserve acquisition and management.

An important element in any legislation is a requirement to produce and disseminate educative information. That aspect particularly has been missing in much of the legislation passed by most European countries.

Additional to the inherent educative role of legislation, is the importance of prosecutions where blatant acts have been committed against bats or their roosts. Obviously, to some extent the legislation has failed if prosecutions are found necessary, but every opportunity should be used to show, through the media, what went wrong, how bats were harmed and, most important, what should be done to avoid similar prosecutions in future. The fines imposed need to be sufficient to act as a deterrent to others, but should not be so high as to shock people into thinking bats are over-protected.

EDUCATION

Arguably, this is the most important aspect of any conservation strategy for bats. For centuries these mysterious animals have been the subject of superstitions or associated with the Devil, and therefore they have been greatly feared. The only way to dispel these misconceptions is through education, and although this need is common to all wildlife conservation, it is especially important for bats because of their dependency on human dwellings.

Materials

Carefully prepared leaflets, inexpensively produced in large numbers, are the most important basic resource. These must be clearly written, giving details about the life history of bats to include information on where they live, their social life, their slow breeding rate and their vulnerability, especially of the nursery and hibernation roosts. They should explain why bats are protected and what people can do to help conserve them. It is preferable to include at least one attractive close-up profile photograph of a bat's head, to show a large open eye and closed mouth. People are not endeared to bats showing teeth! Species usually regarded as being most attractive to human eyes include *Nyctalus, Pipistrellus, Vespertilio* and *Plecotus*, especially if the ears of the latter are fully erect. At the end of the leaflet, contact addresses should be included, to show where additional advice may be obtained and where to send information about bats.

The second level of educative material should be more detailed, dealing with conservation problems and solutions. These can include more leaflets but an audio-visual pack is particularly useful, especially if it includes colour photographs of all species, with examples of where they roost and even solutions to some problems such as cave grilles and bat boxes. Having a slide pack readily available, helps the media such as television and newspapers, who may urgently wish to feature a bat story but only if it can be illustrated. Across Europe there are many excellent examples of this kind of educative material, but sadly a substantial number of States still do not have such publications. Advice in preparing appropriate material is available through the Chiroptera Specialist Group of the Species Survival Commission, IUCN.

Dissemination of Material

Although the production of information leaflets and other educative material is the vital first step, it is of little use until distributed to those who most need it. Leaflets should be widely circulated and freely given to all sections of society, especially to schools, members of the public who have bats in their property and people who in their work may affect bats' lives, such as builders and foresters. If literature is posted to someone who is threatening to destroy bats, the recipient may be illiterate, may not understand the language or dialect in which it is written, may not make the time to read it or may even have an aversion to receiving 'official' papers. In order to be most effective, such information should be delivered by a bat expert who can listen to the problem and provide detailed advice.

It is unrealistic to expect State agencies to employ sufficient staff to undertake all such work. The State can provide the administrative structure and detailed scientific expertise when required, but most important is the need for each country to stimulate, educate and train a network of amateurs who can respond locally to requests for help.

Amateur Bat Groups

As well as solving individual problems, amateurs in bat conservation groups can stimulate and lead education programmes in schools, colleges and the media. These kinds of activities have proved very cost effective in the Netherlands, Switzerland, Great Britain and France. In large countries it is best to form local bat groups. Members need to be trained by experts to ensure uniformity of approach, and the bat groups ought to have a co-ordinating national bat group to act as a forum between the professional agencies and the amateurs.

Having a national bat group, independent of the State conservation agency, can be useful in several ways. Some people do not like to receive advice from 'officialdom' and would rather talk with 'ordinary people'. An amateur enthusiast is a cost effective way of achieving the aims of bat conservation. Also, if amateurs spend their own time and money on their hobby, it makes others realise that bat conservation is not just something the State wishes to impose upon its unwilling citizens, but something which concerns people like themselves.

Another important function of amateur bat groups, is to undertake survey work. Bat roosts are difficult to find and detailed work by local groups can make significant discoveries about the distribution and abundance of species. Research projects may also be carried out by these groups.

Summarising: amateur bat groups are essential if adequate conservation programmes are to be developed in each State.

SITE PROTECTION AND MANAGEMENT

Resources will be limited for all aspects of bat conservation, consequently it is imperative to make wise use of them. At the start of a bat conservation programme much of the budget will be used most effectively in producing and disseminating education materials, but subsequently, site protection and management will consume a larger part of the finance. The on-going requirement is for survey projects. These provide the base-line data from which value judgements are made as to which sites or species are most important and in need of urgent financial support.

The most difficult problem is how to decide where to spend those limited resources. An individual bat colony may occupy more than 100 different roost sites in a year, and forage over many hundreds of square kilometres. To be effective, a conservation programme must involve protecting all the major roosts and near-by feeding habitat. Before such decisions can be taken, detailed research is needed to identify the key elements which are required to ensure survival of a population. Clearly, it is pointless protecting summer roosts if bats will be killed in hibernation, or preserving important feeding habitat if the local nursery site is lost.

Plate 6. Roost boxes for bats to simulate tree holes. These are rapidly adopted by tree dwelling bats if sited in suitable places (photo: R. E. Stebbings).

Due to lack of detailed knowledge about the distribution and status of bats in most countries, it is necessary to follow a broad based conservation policy. While research continues to focus on the specific requirements of individual species, efforts should be made to reduce or remove the more obvious threats to bats. Many of these threats, such as environmental pollution, are common to most wildlife, but some threats, especially to roosts are peculiar to bats.

Roost Protection

Bats are essentially gregarious animals. Most species form nurseries in summer which frequently contain the entire regional population of adult females. Similarly, some hibernacula contain significant proportions of regional populations. Therefore nurseries and some hibernacula should be protected.

Each State should prepare a list of its resident species, with details of the known colonies and their population sizes. From this list, decisions may be taken as to which roosts need protection to ensure an adequate population is safeguarded.

Consideration should be given to the needs of bats in adjacent States, especially for endangered species or those at the edge of their range. As research continues, new information may show a species is more or less abundant than previously thought, and provision must be made in the strategy to enable reassessment of the priorities.

Roosts in Buildings

Throughout Europe colonies of bats in buildings are being killed or excluded. Many of these cases are avoidable, providing due consideration is given to bats. If a building is to be repaired or modernised, it is important to assess at an early stage whether bats use it. This will enable the work, which needs to be planned around them, to proceed with minimal inconvenience. This co-operation is vitally important, because without repairs a building will fall down and be useless to bats. Thus bats need the sympathy of the property owners, and this kind of co-operation generally causes no extra expense. When bats are known to roost in buildings which are to be repaired, care is needed to make certain neither entrances nor the routes bats take to their roosting sites are blocked, as sometimes they roost many metres from their exits.

'Solid' walls of old buildings and bridges. Bats often breed and hibernate inside 'solid' walls. When maintenance or repairs are planned, a bat expert should first inspect the area to be treated to look for signs of bats. Cracks or holes free of dust and cobwebs used regularly by bats, will have other signs, such as oil stains from the fur on the brick or stone, rubbed smooth by the passage of generations of bats. Sometimes pupa cases of bat parasites may be seen stuck inside the holes (often dark brown, one millimetre ovals), as well as the characteristic bat droppings scattered around.

With large buildings repairs may take many years and this provides the opportunity to undertake comprehensive surveys throughout the year. Close co-operation between the bat observer and the stone masons and builders is highly desirable, so that important bat sites are marked as work proceeds.

However, a more difficult problem to solve is the practice of rendering or plastering fissured walls, especially when remote high pressure devices are used. No structure should be treated unless first inspected by a bat expert. If bats are found, the high pressure method should not be used.

Domestic, public and modern buildings. Large numbers of bats use these buildings throughout the year. Nursery colonies are found in walls or roofs and even between or under floors. Great effort should always be made to ensure the safety and continuance of these sites. Only as a last resort should bats be excluded if they are unwanted by the owner. There is rarely justification for excluding bats from public buildings, but some measures may be taken to reduce such nuisances as droppings falling on ancient monuments in churches. Rather than excluding the bats, measures can be taken to prevent droppings falling in these areas.

Cavity wall insulation. Many cavity walls are used by bats throughout the year, and generally it is not possible to inspect the voids prior to filling with insulation. These should never be filled in winter when bats will be in hibernation. Any buildings known to have colonies in summer are best left untreated because of the likelihood of bats being present in winter. If walls need to be insulated the work should be done in summer, after first watching the outside of the building at dusk, to ensure no bats are present.

Timber treatments. Since the 1950s, many millions of buildings across Europe have had remedial timber treatments to kill wood boring insects and to control wood rotting fungi. Most of the treatments have involved spraying mixtures of persistent chemicals onto the affected timbers. These include pesticides which are often highly toxic to bats and other mammals. Domestic animals and even people are known to have died as a result of some of these treatments. Frequently buildings do not need treating, but owners are persuaded to have it done by advertisers, or by those lending money for house purchase. Where bats are likely to be affected:

◻ If only a small area is damaged, timber should be replaced with pre-treated new wood, rather than having a full spray treatment.

◻ If spraying is to be carried out, only chemicals with low mammalian toxicity, should be used, such as the insecticide Permethrin, and boron based fungicides.

◻ Water based emulsions are preferable (and cheaper) to spirit or petroleum formulations.

◻ Spraying should be done when bats are absent.

In the Federal Republic of Germany especially, some timber treatments involve blowing hot air into roof spaces to kill insects. This is an excellent method as there are no persistent after effects, but, as with other treatments, great care must be taken to be certain bats are not present.

Cellars. In many houses, outside access to cellars has been blocked. In order to allow bats to enter it is desirable to have gaps with a minimum dimension of 400 millimetres wide by 100 millimetres high, or to place metal grilles over the entrances, with spaces of 100-150 millimetres between the horizontal bars. The aim should be to allow sufficient air exchange, to achieve a minimum winter temperature no lower than 0° Celsius. Extensive cellars benefit by having a number of entrances, allowing some sheltered areas to remain warm (10° Celsius), while others cool to freezing temperatures. A wide range of temperature regimes will favour their use by a greater variety of bats.

Central heating boilers have been installed in cellars and have sometimes encouraged nursery colonies of bats. Where practical, the heat from the boiler should be confined, so bats may continue to use cool regions for hibernation. Also, if bats roost in the boiler room they should not hang over the boiler or control equipment, because their droppings could interfere with the control mechanisms and thereby present a fire hazard. Wire netting with holes one centimetre diameter, can be used to construct a cage around the boiler and this should extend to the ceiling.

Roosts in tunnels. Both nursing and hibernating bats are found in tunnels of all kinds. Generally, continued use of tunnels by bats is not compatible with other human activities. Decisions need to be taken as to whether particular sites can be left as sanctuaries for bats or whether another use should take precedence. Tunnels to be protected for bats should have barriers preventing unauthorised entry, with explanatory notices.

Many man-made tunnels, including 'Nietoperek Bat Reserve', Poland, and 'Greywell Canal Tunnel', Great Britain, are amongst the most important hibernation sites in northern Europe. Tunnel systems may be enhanced by creating sanctuary areas where bats are never disturbed. However in large systems, such as the more than 30 kilometres of former defence tunnels incorporating the Nietoperek Bat Reserve, certain kinds of low impact use such as tourism may be acceptable in areas of little or no importance to bats. Exploitation of this kind must be done carefully, with the bats' welfare being the prime consideration.

Gates, walls or grilles must be carefully designed and installed to enable the existing internal environment to be maintained or, where sufficient knowledge exists, improved conditions may be provided. Some bats, especially *Rhinolophus* spp., do not like flying through narrow grilles, so trials should be undertaken using temporary materials, before expensive structures are built.

In Europe, there is great expertise in grilling and gating tunnels as well as improving internal conditions. Advice on individual sites can be provided by the Chiroptera Specialist Group, SSC.

Caves and mines. The major difficulties with these sites, concern the often conflicting needs of tourism, safety and nature conservation. Safety aspects must take precedence, but these places can be given protection to prevent the public or livestock coming to harm, while maintaining accessibility to bats and authorised people. Often with large caves or mines multi-use of the system is possible with bats being given some areas as a sanctuary while other activities can occur elsewhere. It is vital to consult with all groups who are interested in access, especially speleologists, and to seek their co-operation. Sites having diverse uses may need a management plan to ensure clarity of individual responsibilities.

Plate 7. A steel grille to protect a mine from disturbance and vandalism. Before protection, 96 hibernating bats had been killed by people in one incident -- involving burning them and shooting with air guns (photo: R. E. Stebbings).

Many caves and mines which are too small or unsuitable for multi-use, should be protected only for bats. Selection of sites will depend on thorough surveys and continued monitoring, and a range of different kinds of caves should be protected. Criteria for site selection will need to be assessed in each geographic region, based on current and historic knowledge, even if its quality is poor. The aim for each species must be to protect all roosts which contain at least five per cent of a colony. However for endangered species, sites with two per cent would warrant protection. Additional to these considerations are those caves or mines which contain a large number of bats of several species. It is not possible to give precise guidance on how many sites might be considered for special protection, but regional criteria will need to be developed. Often important sites are aggregated in limited areas because of local geology, but sites containing significantly higher numbers of bats, or rare species will become priorities.

Apart from the need to protect the major cave and mine sites where disturbance should be strictly controlled, there is a need to educate all cave visitors as to why they should not disturb bats or pollute the caves. If explosives are to be used, bats should not be present.

Mines should always be inspected by bat experts prior to capping. Those with significant numbers of bats will require a grille while others may be blocked. However, some means of escape for the bats, must always be provided because many mines are too large to search thoroughly and bats are often hidden.

Habitat Protection

Satisfactory conservation of bats will require identification of important feeding habitat for individual colonies of bats. This kind of research is urgently needed. Nevertheless, sufficient is known about the general ecology of bats, the distances they fly nightly and the areas they forage over, to be able to identify the kinds of habitats where these species are seen, but little is known of the feeding ranges for many bat species in Europe.

In many parts of Europe, where the countryside is largely under intensive agriculture, there is little which can be done to make a significant improvement for bats. Roosts should be close to a mixture of pasture and woodland, with corridors of similar habitat, preferably along river valleys, leading to larger blocks of woodland. It is known that all bats frequent riparian pasture, woodland and open water, and on cold windy nights preferentially seek such places to feed. Therefore, depending on the size of colonies, protection should be given to sections of riparian habitat radiating from the roost. As a rule, about two hectares should be allowed for each bat, which means a colony of 100 bats in a specially protected roost, would need a strip of land equivalent to 200 metres wide by ten kilometres long. The management of these areas needs to ensure woodland is not reduced in size, though normal commercial felling and replanting could be encouraged. Old trees with holes should not be felled and other trees should be allowed to reach senility. Adjacent pastures and marshlands should not be treated with fertiliser or herbicides but they do need to be grazed. Traditional methods to control noxious weeds should be employed (for example cutting and pulling).

Forests

Throughout Europe deciduous forests have been felled, and when replaced, conifer species are usually grown. This change has had an enormous effect on the variety and abundance of insect life. Also, forests tend to be managed, so trees do not develop. The tree living bats need holes, so policies are required which not only protect specific old trees and allow them to reach natural death, but ensure younger trees are left to grow old. These old trees which are usually 'tidied up' or removed, are crucial to a large number of wildlife species, some of which have become locally extinct due to an insufficient number of old and dying trees to sustain viable populations. One of the most highly threatened habitats is old trees, especially native species.

Agriculture

Over large areas of Europe, landscape is highly degraded. Bats have lost a large amount of their favoured feeding habitats, of small fields surrounded by shelter-providing trees. In such areas it is difficult to see what practical recommendations can be made, which would give bats the types of habitats they require.

There are measures which can be taken to improve habitats. Positive incentives need to be given to farmers to prevent further loss of riparian woodland, marshland and undrained wet pasture. The ideal would be to recreate a network of shelter belts of woodland to link with existing woodland and pasture. Bats use such places for feeding and as corridors between roosts. Shelter belts have several economic advantages, including reducing wind damage to crops and property, maintaining reservoirs of predators which reduce pest damage to crops, providing a source of timber as well as creating aesthetically pleasing areas for recreation.

Pollution

There is a continuing need to reduce or remove all kinds of pollution. Most of the pollutants are well known and some types are disappearing. However, agricultural pesticides are still directly killing bats. If similar kinds of chemicals are to be used, target-specific pesticides are required. The wide-spectrum pesticides such as the organochlorine compounds, particularly DDT, Dieldrin, Lindane and Chlordane, should be phased out.

Drainage

Rivers, marshland and wet pastures are key habitats for bats and other wildlife and are among the most threatened. There is a need for regional or state-wide assessment of these habitats to ensure a representative network remains. Lowland rivers may need periodic dredging, which should be done whenever possible from one bank, allowing the other to develop old trees.

Summary of site protection

Bats are dependent on a range of roosts and habitats in all areas of Europe. Crucial to the survival of bats and other wildlife are the forestry and agricultural policies of each State. Strategic planning of all resources is needed to include provision or maintenance of refuges for all wildlife. Retention of old trees in forests and agricultural habitats, reduction of pollution and prevention of excessive drainage are all key elements, as is the reinstatement of lost habitats. These sorts of problems need addressing at the highest levels in government, to enable a national strategy to be formulated because the overall health of a nation depends on the overall environment.

CREATION OF NEW ROOSTS

Bat Boxes

Early this century the first purpose built roosts for bats were erected in France, with the intention of simulating hollow trees. Since that time thousands of bat boxes have been installed in forests, gardens and parks throughout Europe, and most European bat species except the *Rhinolophidae* have roosted in them. When constructed and sited carefully they are a valuable conservation tool, especially in forestry plantations.

Most bat boxes have thin walls (about 25 millimetres thick), which provide little insulation from cold weather in winter, hence, bats generally use boxes in summer. There is a need to install more boxes, with walls at least 100 millimetres thick, which will be suitable for hibernation.

'Caves' and Tunnels

Recently a few purpose-built underground sites have been designed and constructed, using knowledge of the kinds of environment bats seek for hibernation. Although these structures can be expensive if they are built in isolation, their cost can be negligible if included as part of an engineering project involving earth moving, such as new road construction.

Often, damaged large-section concrete pipes can be placed as a tunnel beneath embankments. The exact design depends upon many factors, but the aim should be to create roosting places and a range of internal temperatures which do not fall below freezing, except near the entrance. As with any conservation project, it is important to monitor these sites to enable future design improvements to be made.

RESEARCH

This is a vital element to all aspects of a conservation strategy. The most important requirement is for surveys to document past and present population sizes and distributions, and especially to monitor the success of conservation measures.

More sophisticated ecological research is also required, to identify the criteria whereby decisions may be made concerning which sites will need protection, and how best to manage them.

Research programmes need to be planned and executed with great care, as they can damage bat populations. All research involving disturbance or handling bats should be licensed by the enforcing agency for the protective legislation. A panel of bat experts should evaluate prospective projects to ensure the work is scientifically sound, will not significantly affect the bat populations (for example, small numbers of common species might be taken for laboratory studies) and will be carried out with the highest humanitarian principles.

Populations

Surveys are required if assessment is to be made of past and present population sizes, and from this knowledge the species status can be judged.

Historic Population Size

Generally throughout Europe there is little documentary evidence of earlier population sizes. A few European studies, which began in the 1930s in central and north western areas, have shown changes, but these were very localised studies. However, some evidence may be gathered by talking to older local people who may remember former colonies, and by methodically searching for likely places. Earlier population sizes may be estimated from a variety of sources.

These include sizes of guano piles, the quantity of guano removed from roosts annually, areas of rock worn by bats' claws and size of clusters witnessed in the past.

Present Day Populations

Surveys are needed to establish the distribution of species and their population sizes. Efforts should be made to estimate numbers for all bat species but some, especially those using tree holes, are difficult to find. Standardised and regular counts can in time give information on population changes and methodologies are being devised which will allow direct comparisons between States.

Three kinds of survey are being devised. Firstly, hibernacula can be visited at the same time each winter where the bats are identified and counted without disturbance. Secondly, numbers of bats can be counted as they emerge from nursery roosts in summer, before the young are weaned. Thirdly, it is possible to assess bat abundance by using a bat detector and microphone, while driving along fixed transects at the same times each year. These and possibly other methods need to be used together if a reasonably accurate picture is to develop of the changing status of bats in Europe.

Roosts

There are many accounts of the places bats are found, but few measurements of their character have been made. Some information has been documented for cave roosting species, mostly in northern Europe, but much more is needed if scientifically sound criteria are to be developed for assessing site importance. Successful creation of new roosts depends upon this knowledge.

Habitats and Food

Some information is already available on where most bat species are seen and caught. However, in most cases we do not know which kinds of habitat and what species of insects are key elements in the survival of individual species. Without this understanding, wrong decisions may be taken when selecting habitat for special protection.

Being small, highly mobile animals capable of flying long distances in the dark, bats present many problems for those wishing to study them. Modern technology is helping enormously with the development of small lights and radio transmitters to attach to bats, and image intensifiers and bat detectors with which to watch and hear them. These techniques are now well established but much further research is necessary if successful bat conservation is to be achieved.

A few studies have shown what bats eat. Inevitably these have been qualitative, because results have been limited to material recognisable in bat droppings. More studies are needed all over Europe to establish a more complete picture of the diet of each species with any regional variation.

Ecological Studies

In order to obtain a complete picture of a species' life history, in-depth ecological studies are essential. These should last at least five years. It is only by having an integrated and wide-ranging study into the population dynamics, social behaviour, breeding, roost and habitat selection, food and feeding habitats and causes of mortality, that a full understanding of the conservation needs of a species will be identified.

Ringing and marking studies

Marking bats with rings is thought to have caused high mortality in some populations. The causes appeared to be two-fold. Firstly the rings generally were made of soft, sharp-edged aluminium. Chewing by the bats produced jagged edges which caused tears and infection to the membranes and forearm. Frequently the rings were too small for the bat and consequently when inflammation and swelling occurred, the blood supply was restricted. Secondly, marked bats were often over-disturbed, causing them to lose fat reserves and death by starvation ensued.

Project proposals which include ringing bats should be designed to continue for a minimum of three seasons. An initial trial will show whether the bats are suffering damage, and allows the possibility of rings being removed if found necessary because of ring damage. But any studies where ringing is proposed, must be carefully considered to ensure no other method will produce the required results. The only rings which should be permitted are those specially designed for bats, made of hard alloys such as 'incaloy' or magnesium and with an entirely smooth, polished surface.

Causes of Mortality

Studies to find the causes of deaths in bats are required to assess the significance of natural mortality, as opposed to man-made incidents. Although some deaths have been attributed to pesticides, no thorough study has been made of the lethal and particularly the sub-lethal effects of these chemicals on bats. This applies equally to chemicals used in forestry, agriculture and timber treatment industries. Because bats are protected and classed as threatened animals, research should be conducted to compare how closely bats and laboratory-bred animals respond. It may be necessary only to do research on laboratory animals and by modelling the data, the results may be related to bats.

Although little is known, natural diseases are probably a major cause of bat mortality. Cross infection between bats and other animals is unlikely, but some research is needed on this topic. Perhaps most important is the necessity to survey the extent of the rabies-like virus in European bats, particularly to discover whether that virus can be transmitted to other animals in the wild. Also research should be conducted to establish how the virus is maintained and how it affects the survival of populations.

CO-ORDINATION OF RESEARCH AND ADVICE

Resources for bat research in Europe are limited and duplication of effort should be avoided. European bat research workers already have a bi- or tri-annual Symposium, which is a forum where ideas are exchanged, and new techniques demonstrated. There is already a strong conservation movement amongst scientists, which has developed since the second International Bat Research Conference held in Amsterdam in 1970. The Chiroptera Specialist Group of the SSC is able to provide advice and assistance on any aspects of research to States and individuals.

Plate 8. Old buildings often contain a variety of bats and require careful renovation and maintenance if bats are to survive in them.

Annex 1
Checklist of the Conservation Needs for European Bats

1. LEGISLATION

No European country has passed fully adequate legislation

- Six states have no laws protecting bats

The form of words in legislation is important

Protection is needed for:

- Bats
- Roosts -- especially all nurseries, and prevention of disturbance
- Feeding habitat

Licensing of:

- Research involving disturbance, handling, marking, taking into captivity
- Filming and photography, in situ or in captivity
- Problem solving (bat roost visitors), for example bats in houses
- Bat removal because of damage to property

2. IMPLEMENTATION

Appoint State agency or National authority.

Agency needs budget and staff for:

- Administration
- Field officers
- Reserves and management

- Research
- Education
- Prosecutions

3. EDUCATION

3.1 Materials

- Leaflets: General, natural history and conservation
- Special topics, for example, grilling caves, bat boxes, house bats
- Posters/stickers
- Audio-visual slides and videos
- Films, books, sales goods

3.2 Dissemination of material

- Centrally from governmental or non-government agency
- To other government departments especially forestry and agriculture
- To builders/timber preservation specialists
- To pest control organisations
- To amateur bat groups
- To general public

3.3 Amateur bat groups should be encouraged by State agency. They are cost-effective for bat conservation to help with:

- Education, survey, research projects
- Need training and co-ordination by national group/interfaced with State agency
- Sometimes more effective than State agency, because seen to be 'ordinary people' -- not 'official'

4. SITE PROTECTION AND MANAGEMENT

- Surveys to document sites/numbers of bats/species
- Development of criteria to allow selection of sites to be protected
- One colony needs protection of summer and winter roosts as well as key feeding areas
- Endangered species need special consideration

4.1 Roost protection

- Especially all nurseries
- For rare/endangered species, due consideration should be given to status in adjacent States

4.1.1 Roosts in buildings

- Check if bats present before repairs or alterations
- Register site with State agency
- Seek advice
- Plan work accordingly

4.1.1.1 Old buildings and bridges

- 'Solid' walls are very important for nurseries and hibernation roosts
- Bat expert should **always** inspect before repairs
- Leave crevices/holes for bat access

4.1.1.2 Cavity wall insulation

- Never insulate in winter
- Buildings with known colonies -- preferably do not fill, otherwise check in summer, if no bats emerge fill immediately

4.1.1.3 Timber treatments

- Only if needed
- Mechanical replacement of timber -- best solution.
- Otherwise hot air when bats absent -- best, non-persistent sprays -- use low mammalian toxicity -- water based formulations

4.1.1.4 Cellars

- Grille entrance if required for security
- Closed cellars -- open and grille -- adjust temperature regime

4.1.2 Roosts in tunnels (nurseries and hibernalcula)

- Bat/human use often not compatible, for example railway tunnels for shooting range
- Large systems may have multi-users, for example defence systems

. Protect important sites with grilles
. Liaise with other interested parties for time-sharing

4.1.3 Caves and mines

Safety/protection measures needed

. Caves:
    * Keep some as sanctuaries
    * Large systems, multi-use may be possible but some areas designated as sanctuaries
. Mine capping: always inspect before capping -- leave gap for bats to escape
. Grille mines important for bats
. Grilles need careful planning to avoid excluding bats
. Protect range of cave/mine types in each area
. Criteria for site protection need to be developed for each State
. Guideline criteria
. Endangered species sites
    * Those which regularly shelter two per cent of the individuals of a colony of one species
. Other species sites
    * Those which regularly shelter 100 bats or five per cent of a State or regional population of one species

4.1.4 Trees

. Old trees to be protected especially those with holes

4.2 Habitat protection

. Major feeding habitats
. Corridors of riparian or other woodland and pasture radiating from important nursery and other roosts
. Network of woodlands/shelter belts are needed for inter-roost movements
. Two hectares per bat should be protected near to specially protected roosts, for example for endangered species

4.2.1 Forests

. Young trees should be designated to remain to senility
. Replant deciduous woodlands with native trees -- protect remaining stock

4.2.2. Agriculture

- Planting of shelter belts of woodlands in denuded prairie-style landscape
- Safeguard marshlands, wet pasture, riparian woodland and all broad-leaved woodland

4.2.3 Pollution

- Reduce/prevent agricultural/industrial pollutants including fertilisers, herbicides, pesticides, slurry, sewage, silage
- Encourage development of target specific means of controlling pests

4.2.4 Drainage

- Rivers, marshland, wet pastures need protection -- these areas countrywide -- ensure adequate remains protected
- Do river maintenance from one bank -- old trees to remain on other side

4.3 Co-ordination within State government departments

- Conservation of habitat needs to have as strong a voice as departments of forestry and agriculture
- Maintenance of healthy environment -- in widest sense -- is vital to human survival and well-being, as well as for bats

5 CREATION OF NEW ROOSTS

5.1 Bat boxes

- Summer and winter style boxes are a useful conservation tool

5.2 Caves and tunnels

- Adapt existing to provide suitable conditions for bats
- Open up blocked caves/mines/tunnels
- Create bat roost tunnels as part of road development schemes

6 RESEARCH

- Successful conservation is dependent on research
- Essential to monitor success of conservation programmes

. Needs to be carefully planned to avoid killing bats
. Needs to avoid duplication of effort

6.1 Populations

6.1.1 Historic population sizes

. From documentary evidence and estimated from various sources
. Surveys to find former breeding sites

6.1.2 Present day populations

. Continuing long-term research to:
  * Survey and document location/type of sites
  * Research to estimate population sizes
. Use of standardised internationally agreed methods

6.2 Roosts

. Characterisation of roosts is needed to allow successful modification or creation of new sites
. Evaluate roost selection, per species in relation to habitat

6.3 Habitats and food Requirements:

. Identification and characterisation of feeding habitats for each species -- how do they vary across Europe?
. Qualitative identification of prey species for each bat species

6.4 Autecological studies

. In-depth research into the population ecology of representative species is needed, so that scientifically sound conservation may be formulated

6.5 Causes of mortality

. Some bat mortality may be prevented if detailed research examines causes
. Further work needs to be done on the rabies-type virus in bats
  * How does it affect bat survival?
  * Can it be transmitted to other wildlife in the field?

6.6 Ringing and marking studies

. Some methods have been very damaging to bats
. Only well planned projects should involve ringing

- Only purpose made rings of good proven design and materials must be used
- There should be an international agreement on standards

6.7 Migrations

- Collate information
- Assess need for special studies

7 CO-OPERATION

- The bi-annual European Bat Research Symposia already exists as a forum to exchange information
- The SSC Chiroptera Specialist Group can co-ordinate, assist and advise

8 DEVELOPMENT OF CONSERVATION STRATEGIES FOR ENDANGERED SPECIES

- Endangered species are priorities for conservation
- Full scale projects are needed, involving where appropriate, international co-operation
- See example in Annex 2

*Plate 9. The greater horseshoe bat, **Rhinolophus ferrumequinum**, is now very rare or extinct in many areas, especially in north west Europe, and is in serious decline everywhere.*

Annex 2
Development of a Conservation Strategy for an Endangered Species: an Example

In order to prevent the extinction of a species it is necessary to formulate and follow through a conservation strategy. Because these plans take time to develop, adequate protective measures for the most important sites will be needed at an early stage.

None of the 30 European bat species have their range entirely within Europe. Nevertheless, there have been some local extinctions caused by human activities. In those areas where the contiguous range of an endangered species spans two or more States, a conservation strategy should be developed with consultation between those States. These are the ideals embodied in the 'Bonn Convention'. Under the terms of this Convention 'An AGREEMENT on the Conservation of Bats in Europe' has been formulated, and hopefully all states in Europe will accede to it.

Some populations of endangered species are isolated and if these occur entirely within one state, conservation strategies can be developed specifically for them. In Great Britain, several bat species may interchange with populations in mainland Europe, but the two *Rhinolophus* species do not.

An outline conservation strategy is given here for the most highly endangered species *R. ferrumequinum*.

CONSERVATION OF *R. FERRUMEQUINUM* IN GREAT BRITAIN

History

The possibility of substantial declines in the population of *R. ferrumequinum* in Great Britain having occurred this century was

70

first considered in 1961. Two sources of evidence led to this conclusion. Firstly, a building was discovered which formerly housed a large colony. It had been treated with the pesticide Lindane to kill wood boring beetles and as a result, an estimated 15,000 bats were killed. Secondly, documentary reports showed the species previously occurred in areas where now they were absent.

The discovery of further documentation, combined with site visits, showed that the species no longer lived in about half the range occupied in the early 1900s. Of 17 nursery roost sites known, by 1961 only four were still used.

Survey and Research

R. ferrumequinum had disappeared from many roosts, but it was also known the species occurred over most of south west England and Wales. This wide distribution suggested it was likely there were other nurseries. Clusters of up to 100 bats were found in hibernation in some areas far from known nurseries. Nationally at that time about 300 winter roosts were known, including caves, mines and buildings.

Surveys were conducted in likely areas. These involved searching maps for features such as caves, mines, tunnels, fortifications and large estate buildings, and site visits were then made. Many roosts were discovered as a result of information received following appeals in newspapers, and on radio or television.

A few former roosts were found when piles of droppings were discovered in buildings due for renovation. In recent years such sites have been notified to the Nature Conservancy Council (NCC) as is required by the Wildlife and Countryside Act 1981. By 1987, a total of 58 nursery sites had been identified but only 14 of these were still in use. Undoubtedly, others remain undiscovered.

R. ferrumequinum is now known to have used over 600 roosts but formerly there were probably three or four times that number and many will have been destroyed.

Bats in four colonies were studied by marking individuals with rings. Two studies lasted from 1947 to 1960 and from 1976 to 1982, and two begun in 1955 and 1956 continue to the present.

These research studies have provided basic information on population size, structure, and breeding rate. They allow estimates to be made of population sizes when only the numbers of births are known, also they have revealed daily and annual home ranges and social behaviour in roosts.

Seasonal changes in guano production per bat have been measured, and compared with areas and volumes of guano piles in sites no longer used by bats. This can be used to estimate former colony size. Microscopic identification of insect remains in droppings allows interpretation of which months a disused roost was occupied, and hence whether it was likely to have been a nursery. Cave nursery roosts sometimes show domes of erosion, where bat claws have worn away the rock. This can indicate the long term usage and importance of the site, and, combined with other information can allow estimates of former numbers.

Causes of the Decline

In some cases there is an obvious cause of the loss of a colony. Fires destroyed two nursery colonies, and pesticides killed six. Two of the latter were deliberate acts against bats and the others were the result of remedial timber treatments. Other losses were caused by exclusion of colonies (perhaps involving killing), destruction of the roost, frequent disturbance of bats, and six colonies declined for no known reason. In each case there was likely to be several contributory causes, but catastrophic loss due to single events, is believed to have caused the death of several tens of thousands of bats, many since 1950. Of 45 former nursery colonies, it is thought ten were lost before 1910, eight more up to 1950, a further 14 to 1970 and another 13 by 1987.

Hibernation sites generally shelter small numbers of bats from one colony, but gradual loss of such places, combined with acts of vandalism involving killing bats, have contributed to the declines. In one small area of Dorset, England, about 80 hibernation sites were lost in the 1950s by filling entrances to tunnels. Some bats would have been trapped inside and killed in this way. Similar losses have occurred in all areas.

Detailed research into the bats food and feeding habits involved marking them with radio transmitters. This technique revealed their foraging areas and hitherto unknown roosts. It also allowed an appraisal to be made of the importance of differing habitats and how the bats needs varied seasonally. On cold spring nights, insects emerge from pasture and fly to warmer woodland, where bats catch them. However in summer, bats prefer to feed over pasture and catch mostly dung beetles and noctuid moths. Bats also need open areas of water where they can drink, especially on hot days. Woodland and permanent pasture are habitats which have declined greatly, both in area and quality. Almost certainly these losses have substantially affected bat survival and contributed to their decline.

These bats, like many species are very sensitive to disturbance at their roosts. At present there is too much disturbance in both summer and hibernation sites, and apart from two on-going research projects there is a need to create all other important sites into sanctuaries. Indeed disturbance by naturalists has been a contributory cause of declines.

WHAT KIND OF STRATEGY IS NEEDED

By pooling all available information an estimate was derived which suggested the population in Great Britain in the late nineteenth century would have numbered 300,000 bats. The estimate in 1987 was 3,000 bats, and they produced about 700 young. Thus, of the number estimated for the turn of this century, only about one per cent of *R. ferrumequinum* remain in 1987. The decline is due to several causes, including accidental and deliberate killing and loss of habitat. Many of these problems can be avoided or prevented.

Legislation

R. ferrumequinum was one of two bat species given protection in 1975, under the Wild Creatures and Wild Plants Act. However, their roosts were not given protection, nor was it an offence to disturb the the animals. In 1981, under the Wildlife and Countryside Act, deliberate disturbance became illegal, together with intentional damage to bats or their roosts. These laws have had considerable beneficial affects on bat conservation, but are far from perfect. For instance it is difficult to prove 'intent' to damage or destroy bats or their roosts, so roosts may be lost and bats killed without a punishable offence being committed. The legislation makes provision for roosts or habitats to be given special protection as Sites of Special Scientific Interest (SSSI), or as nature reserves. SSSIs are notified to the owner with a list of actions which would harm the site and which should not be done without obtaining the agreement of the NCC. In practise, this kind of protection has limited success in preventing degradation or loss of sites.

There is a need for better legislation to give stronger protection to bat roosts, especially of endangered species, and to significant areas of habitat around specially protected nursery roosts. Firstly, the legislation needs alteration to replace the word '...intentionally...' with 'recklessly', and secondly, to ensure buildings containing endangered species receive specific protection.

Research and Survey

Research is a vital component of any conservation project. The most basic needs are to conduct surveys to find roosts and make systematic counts of bats. This kind of information is required to enable the monitoring of population sizes subsequent to conservation measures. In Great Britain there is a need for more accurate monitoring of each colony, of adults and births, as only major changes may be detected with present levels of observation.

Site Protection

Nurseries

All sites should be specially protected where five or more young are born each year. Therefore, twelve of the 14 currently known nurseries need special protection, and in fact some of this has already been done by designations as SSSIs. One of the major problems arises because, with one exception, the nurseries are in buildings, seven of which are in use by the owners. In order to protect the remaining population of this species in Great Britain, it is essential to ensure all remaining nurseries are not further degraded, either in the size of the roost space or the quality of adjacent feeding habitat.

Hibernacula and Other Roosts

A single colony needs many different kinds of roosts. Research has shown that bats have requirements which vary seasonally, and according to the different age, sex, weight and classes and experience. Individual adult males occupy traditional roosts throughout the year and these are used for mating. An adequate range of roosts require special protection, especially as one colony may be scattered over many hundreds of square kilometres.

In practice, special protection should be given to all sites visited by 50 or more individual bats in one season, or 20 per cent of a colony, whichever is less. However, this knowledge can only be gained by detailed population studies involving mark and recapture.

Defining 'site' is important in this context. With large caves and mines which have several kilometres of passage and a number of entrances, a 'site' could be a part of those systems. Where there are a number of small roost sites in a local area, each having a few tens of metres of tunnel, with a group of bats moving between them, they may be regarded collectively as 'one site'. Only detailed research will identify the importance of each such 'site'.

A number of mating roosts should be protected as they too, are vital for the survival of each colony. It is not known how many are required, but at least five sites need protection for every 100 members of a colony.

Apart from legal protection, all sites need physical barriers, particularly grilles, which have to be very carefully designed and positioned. Badly built grilles have deterred bats.

Habitat Protection

Research has shown the importance of unimproved pasture and woodland close to nursery and other important summer roosts. Most feeding occurs within eight kilometres of the roosts.

R. ferrumequinum need a minimum of about two hectares of woodland and pasture per bat radiating from the roost. With a species so critically endangered, it is important to clearly identify actual feeding habitat, and this will need research in each area.

Creative Conservation

Almost all remaining colonies are in decline and unless positive measures are taken, further colony loss is to be expected with more fragmentation of populations. Creating sanctuaries for the species is possibly the only way to reverse the trend.

In south Devon, a sanctuary was created for the largest nursery colony in Britain, which occupied a derelict building and caves a few metres away. The building was purchased and rebuilt in winter when the bats were hibernating in the nearby caves and elsewhere. Subsequently, the bats were not disturbed, and within seven years a threefold increase in numbers was recorded. At this time other roosts became disused and it appears bats from many scattered sites gathered at the sanctuary. Disturbance in these other sites was the likely cause of bats vacating.

Another site, in Dorset, was rebuilt specifically for the bats and various new areas were created for them. The bats now have dark secluded rooms and passages, which they use mostly through the night before returning to the roof by day. They fly for long periods in these areas, and food is often taken in to feeding perches to be consumed. The use of these new spaces enables some bats to remain in the building throughout the year. Heaters maintained at 30 degrees Celsius have been installed in the roof to provide optimum conditions for bats, resulting in improved breeding success.

R. ferrumequinum prefer nursery sites which incorporate warm areas, for example beneath black slate roofs, and cool tunnels or cellars where they can become torpid and conserve energy. Prior to leaving roosts, bats like to fly extensively and in seclusion, around a large volume, before flying directly into woodland. They do not like flying in open areas until it is dark. All these conditions need to be provided in the surviving nursery roosts.

SUMMARY

Nursery roosts of *R. ferrumequinum* require large volumes in which they can fly in seclusion; a variety of roosting chambers providing differing environmental conditions; and a cold cave, tunnel or cellar within a few metres. They need scrub, old pasture and woodland around the roost with open water near by.

Approximately two hectares per bat of pasture and woodland should be protected near the roosts. The bats should not be disturbed in any sites except when detailed, clearly defined research is necessary.

All important roosts, visited by 20 per cent of a colony or more, should receive special protection, as well as five mating roosts for every 100 bats in each colony.

Development Stages in the Conservation of Endangered Species

Priority order

1) Protect known roost sites

2) Ensure legislation is adequate

3) Do surveys of present and historic roosts/populations.

4) Undertake clearly defined research to answer key questions, for example:

- What is the distribution and number of nurseries?

- How many bats are there in nurseries?

- Where do they hibernate?

- What other roosts are used?

- Where do they feed?

- What do they eat?

- How far do they range daily/annually?

5) Do an in-depth study of population dynamics of at least one colony, to establish age to breeding, reproductive rate, sex ratio, mortality rate and when mortality occurs.

Part Two

Country Accounts

Introduction

The following are accounts of the conservation status of bats in each European country. The differing lengths of account, to some extent, reflect the scientific knowledge of bats and conservation awareness in those States, but also they illustrate the differing problems faced in the various regions. Accounts have not been received from a number of States.

In the accounts, contact addresses are given wherever possible to enable more detailed information to be obtained direct, if required. All the scientists who have supplied information for these reports, are listed in the acknowledgements. The information presented here is to be updated regularly, and the author will be pleased to receive corrections and new information.

Inevitably, the information relating to achievements will need constant updating, but one of the purposes of describing work in each country is to provide inspiration for others. With improved communications between States, and the rapid advance in techniques and technology, acquisition of knowledge, assessment of problems and implementation of conservation proposals will be more quickly and efficiently achieved.

Categories Used to Indicate the Status of Species

The following Red Data Book categories designated by the Species Survival Commission of IUCN, are used throughout the

Figure 3. Map showing the locations of States included in the country accounts. The numbers refer to chapters.

4	Denmark	21	Isle of Man
5	Norway	22	Guernsey
6	Sweden	23	Jersey
7	Finland	24	Portugal
8	Estonia SSR	25	Gibraltar
9	Latvia SSR	26	Spain
10	Lithuania SSR	27	France
11	Poland	28	Switzerland and Leichtenstein
12	Czechoslovakia	29	Italy
13	Democratic Republic of Germany	30	Austria
14	Federal Republic of Germany	31	Hungary
15	Netherlands	32	Yugoslavia
16	Belgium	33	Romania
17	Luxembourg	34	Bulgaria
18	Great Britain	35	Greece
19	Northern Ireland	36	Albania
20	Eire	37	Malta

accounts. Where local variations exist, they are mentioned in the appropriate country account.

Extinct (Ex)

Species not found in the wild during the past 50 years.

Endangered (E)

Species in danger of extinction and whose survival is unlikely if the causal factors continue operating. Included are taxa whose numbers have been reduced to a critical level or whose habitats have been so drastically reduced that they are deemed to be in immediate danger of extinction.

Vulnerable (V)

Species believed likely to move into the Endangered category in the near future if the causal factors continue operating

Rare (R)

Species with small known populations which are not at present Endangered or Vulnerable, but are at risk. These taxa are usually localised within geographical areas or habitats, or are thinly scattered over a more extensive range.

Indeterminate (I)

Species *known* to be Extinct, Endangered, Vulnerable or Rare, where there is insufficient information to state which of the four categories is appropriate.

Insufficiently known (K)

Species which are *suspected* but not definitely known to belong to any of the above categories, because of lack of information.

Not threatened (Nt)

Species which are neither rare nor threatened.

4
Denmark

A Bat Project organised by Dr. Hans Baagoe of the Zoological Museum, has been in operation since 1980. It aims to find the distribution and status of Danish bats, their choice of habitats and relationship with man. Two methods are used.

Firstly, searches for bat roosts based on contacts with the public:

- By advertising for information about bat roosts, through articles in newspapers, radio and television.

- Requesting complaints about bats be directed to the Zoological Museum where people can obtain information and help.

- Analysing bats found weak or dead, for a bat related rabies virus which was first discovered in Denmark in 1985.

Secondly, as all Scandinavian bat species can be identified in the field with bat detectors (except for *Myotis mystacinus* and *brandtii*, which are recorded as *M. mystacinus/brandtii*), this is a very efficient way of monitoring.

Bats are monitored in 10 x 10 kilometer UTM grid squares, both by driving through the area with a microphone mounted on the roof of a car and by walking in selected areas with detectors. Between 1981 and 1987 representative areas were visited in the whole of Zealand, Bornholm, Lolland, Falster and Funen and in north, mid and southern Jutland. This project is continuing.

Danish Bats and their Status

Scientific and Local Name	Frequency of Occurrence*	Status
Myotis mystacinus (Skaegflagermus)	Common on Bornholm Absent elsewhere	V
Myotis brandtii (Brandts flagermus)	Common on Bornholm Fairly rare elsewhere	V
Myotis daubentonii (Vandflagermus)	Common: Large hibernating populations in Jutland	V
Myotis dasycneme (Damflagermus)	Small summer and winter populations in mid-Jutland Otherwise rare	E
Myotis nattereri (Frynseflagermus)	Rare	V
Pipistrellus pipistrellus (Dvaergflagermus)	Very common	Nt
Pipistrellus nathusii (Troldflagermus)	Fairly rare	R
Eptesicus serotinus (Sydflagermus)	Very common: Large populations especially in Jutland	--
Eptesicus nilssonii (Nordflagermus)	Probably not resident but possibly vagrant	Nt
Vespertilio murinus (Skimmelflagermus)	Very common: Large population in N E Zealand	V
Nyctalus noctula (Brunflagermus)	Common in wooded areas and parks	V
Plecotus auritus (Langoret flagermus)	Common	V
Barbastella barbastellus (Bredoret flagermus)	Very rare	R

* The abundance scale is a relative scale for bats only and has no validity in comparison to other animal categories. A 'very common' bat species may still be vulnerable.

Feeding Habitats

Varied landscape with woods, scattered groups of trees, parks and open areas, together with ponds, lakes and rivers, are optimal hunting areas for most Danish bat species. A mosaic of habitat types support an abundant and wide variety of insects, on which the bats feed.

A few bat species are also found in urban areas with an abundance of trees and gardens, for example *P. pipistrellus* and *E. serotinus*, and some exploit the large number of insects which are attracted to bright street lamps in late summer and autumn, for example, *V. murinus, E. serotinus* and *N. noctula*.

Several species hunt near trees, forest edges and even amongst branches (*P. auritus, M. nattereri*), while *V. murinus* and *N. noctula* prefer open areas. Insects emerging from water (rivers, lakes and ponds) are vital for some species, like *M. daubentonii* and *M. dasycneme*, but other species feed in riparian habitat especially in spring.

Roosts

Summer Roosts

Buildings, especially houses, are vital for *V. murinus, E. serotinus, P. pipistrellus, P. nathusii, M. dasycneme, M. nattereri, M. mystacinus* and *M. brandtii*. Most species are found in well ventilated and insulated modern family houses for instance *V. murinus, E. serotinus* and *P. pipistrellus*.

N. noctula and *M. daubentonii* appear to be dependent on hollow trees.

Winter Roosts

Well insulated houses, often with hollow walls are vital winter roosts for *E. serotinus* and *P. pipistrellus*, while tall, five to thirty storey city buildings are used by *V. murinus*. *N. noctula* use hollow trees and the *Myotis* species depend on caves, mines and cellars.

Threats

The general impoverishment of the landscape including water-ways, results in a poorer diversity of habitats, and is believed to be the major threat for many species. However, species which exploit all kinds of habitat, such as *E. serotinus* and *P. pipistrellus* may not suffer declines because of this.

Forestry policies involving the felling of old trees threaten species such as *N. noctula* and *M. daubentonii* and many others.

A growing tendency to retain some old hollow trees is good, but there is no policy for allowing the development of hollows in trees. There is a tendency to fell trees showing the early stages of decay or if they are damaged, as they are regarded as potentially of no commercial value as timber. Small bat boxes are only a partial substitute for hollow trees because they do not provide enough insulation to allow them to serve as winter quarters.

Destruction of winter roosts such as caves, is a potential threat, but in Denmark is not critical at the moment.

Exclusion of bats from houses may be a threat to some species especially *M. dasysneme*, but there is a growing awareness amongst the public that bats should be left undisturbed in these sites.

Discovery of a rabies-like virus in Danish bats (mainly in *E. serotinus*), greatly increased the number of enquiries from people concerned about the risks involved, and who were seeking advice. Hysteria has been avoided and many people have accepted that the bats should stay in their houses even if one or two rabid bats were found beneath the roost. This acceptance is due largely to the excellent education carried out by bat biologists and veterinary officers in conjunction with the quality press.

Also, the Danish public show a high level of understanding for nature and natural diversity.

Key Sites

Important hibernacula for *Myotis* species are the Jutland lime-stone mines. Estimates of the number of bats dependent on the large Monsted mine are: *M. daubentonii* 4,500-5,000, *M. dasycneme* 700-800, *M. brandti* 50-70, with a few *M. nattereri* and

P. auritus. Similar numbers of each species are found in the nearby Daugbjerg mine.

Two small caves at Tingbaek, together contain about 500 bats and one at Smidie about 700, but in these mines there are more *M. brandtii* and *M. nattereri*, in addition to some *M. daubentonii* and *M. dasycneme.* A mine at Alborg contains about 100 *M. daubentonii* in hibernation.

In winter the Jutland limestone mines contain some of the largest populations of hibernating bats in western Europe and they are vital for the survival of the west European population of the endangered *M. dasycneme.*

Protected Sites

The small Smidie limestone mine is a State nature reserve, protected by law and now grilled. The large Monsted mine in privately owned and is not protected. The owner cooperates with the State authorities and always seeks professional advice before undertaking changes in management. Daugbjerg limestone mine is also privately owned but has been protected by declaration since 1951. At Tingbaek, two small mines are privately owned and the Aelborg tunnel is municipally owned, but none of these three are protected.

Although these important mines vary as to their ownership and protection, none of them are immediately threatened as hibernacula for bats. Most of them have locked gates. Admittance is controlled and limited to certain sections, and in some cases, only in the summer.

Bat researchers constantly maintain contact with mine owners, and their advice is always sought when management changes are planned. However, the situation may quickly change and immediate action to protect sites may become necessary.

All the mines are important and all must be protected.

Creation of New Roost Sites

A partly collapsed chalk mine in Jutland has recently been opened and grilled, but no attempt has been made to create new 'caves'.

Conservation of Endangered Species

In Denmark, only one species is classified as endangered -- *M. dasycneme*. It was realised only in the last ten years how important the Jutland area was for this species. Nothing is known about former population sizes. Worldwide the species appears to have three major foci, Denmark-Netherlands, the southern Urals and around Leningrad. Since all known populations, except the Danish have declined substantially, the species requires special consideration.

A conservation strategy requires that all important roosts and feeding habitats be identified and protected. Roosts with 50 or more bats should be given full legal protection. Funding will be required to undertake adequate research to enable identification of key sites with further funding for legal and protective measures.

This is a priority project for Denmark and Europe.

Legislation - Conservation Measures

In Denmark, all bats have been protected by law since 1931 (Game Act of 1931). Since the Game Act of 1967, all mammals and birds which are not mentioned as having an open season are fully protected and must not be hunted and killed. Furthermore it is forbidden to ring or mark bats without a licence. Sometimes bats are a nuisance (real or imaginary) in houses, and people seek means to be rid of them without actually breaking the law. Appropriate advice is given by the biologists. However, education programmes, in conjunction with coverage of the bat-virus situation, have had the effect of bringing people who come across bats to seek professional advice before taking action. New measures are needed to protect bat roosts, especially the nurseries.

Education

Information about bats is disseminated through articles in magazines, newspapers and radio and television programmes. A booklet about bats as threatened animals was recently published for circulation to the public.

The Danes are reasonably well informed about bats, probably because of the extensive press coverage of the bat virus situation. In these press releases bat conservationists were able to broadcast balanced information, including the fact that bats are threatened species which should be left alone in their normally inaccessible roosting sites in buildings.

Research

Numbers of bats hibernating in the Jutland limestone mines, are recorded annually by manual counts and by automatic recording equipment.

The bat project of the Zoological Museum, Universitetsparken 15, DK2100 Copenhagen, will be continued and will also include regular checks of important summer roosts and areas where bats congregate to forage. It is particularly important to undertake an ecological study of *M. dasycneme*, and although one is planned, it requires funding. Detailed knowledge of this endangered species is necessary if its future is to be secure.

Most bat work in Denmark is undertaken by a few professional bat researchers and a small number of amateurs. There is a need to encourage more amateurs to help with counts outside important roosts, and conservation work.

Bibliography

• Baagoe, H.J. (1981) Danish bats, status and protection, *Myotis*, 18-19, 16-18, Bonn.

• Baagoe, H.J. (1983) *Flagermus, Truede Dyr i Danmark.* Danmarks Naturfredningsforenings Forlag. 32 pp. Copenagen.

• Baagoe, H.J. (1986) Summer occurrence of *Vespertilio murinus* (Linné, 1758) and *Eptesicus serotinus* (Schreber, 1780) (Chiroptera, Mammalia) on Zealand, Denmark, based on records of roosts and registrations with bat detectors *Ann. Naturhist, Mus. Wien*, 88/89B, 281-291.

• Grauballe, P.C., Baagoe, H.J., Fekadu, M., Westergaard, J.M. and Zoffmann, H., (1987) Bat Rabies in Denmark. *The Lancet* (1987) 379-380.

5

Norway

There has been no major study of the bats in Norway and hence knowledge of the distribution and abundance of all species is poor. A few notes have been published on the distribution of bats, but there has been no systematic searching for bats or their roosts.

Nine species have been recorded and a tenth, *Nyctalus noctula* has been reported but not confirmed. At least a further two may occur, *Myotis dasycneme* and *Eptesicus serotinus*, as they are found in southern Sweden.

The extent to which Norwegian bats migrate south to hibernate, is unknown, but there is no winter record for *Pipistrellus pipistrellus*. However, in autumn some vagrant bats have been found in Scotland and on North Sea oil platforms, usually coincidental with strong north east winds from the direction of Norway.

Roosts

Summer Roosts

Large nursery colonies of *P. pipistrellus* are known in buildings. One farm building contained two colonies, the other species being *Eptesicus nilssonii*.

Winter Roosts

Bats are rarely found in hibernation, but a few mines contain small numbers of at least five species.

Norwegian Bats and their Status

Scientific and Local Name	Frequency of Occurrence	Status
Myotis mystacinus (Skjeggflaggermus)	Common and widespread	Nt
Myotis brandtii (Brandtflaggermus)	Only one record but probably widespread	?
Myotis daubentonii (Vannflaggermus)	Common and widespread	Nt
Myotis nattereri (Borsteflaggermus)	Only a few records from south east	R
Pipistrellus pipistrellus (Dvergflaggermus)	Locally common especially in south west	Nt
Eptesicus nilssonii (Nordflaggermus)	The most common and widespread species	Nt
Vespertilio murinus (Skimmelflaggermus)	A few records from the Oslo area	R
Nyctalus noctula (Storflaggermus)	Likely occurrence but unsubstantiated	--
Plecotus auritus (Langoreflaggermus)	Common and widespread	Nt
Barbastella barbastellus (Bredoreflaggermus)	Only a few records from south east	R

Threats

Despite being protected, 50 to 100 adult female *P. pipistrellus* with about 100 young, were removed from a factory because they were considered to be a nuisance. Almost certainly some of the young will have died. In Autumn 1985, several thousand bats of the same species entered a private dwelling. Instead of allowing the animals to leave, the Directorate for Nature Conservation permitted the gassing of the colony.

Legislation - Conservation Measures

Bats were given protection under the Wildlife Act (Lov 29, mai 1981 nr 38 om viltet), with amendments of 8 April 1983. It is general wildlife legislation, in which bats are not specifically named, but nevertheless are protected. It is illegal to capture or kill bats, and the roosts also are given protection.

However, effectively there has been no implementation of the legislation for bats, with no circulation of specific education material. It appears some adherence to the law has been practiced by pest control companies, some of whom have refused to respond to requests to kill bats.

Norway has ratified both the Bern and Bonn Conventions and therefore the State has indicated its intention to implement essential conservation measures for bats.

Education and Research

Much work is needed to produce and disseminate literature about bats. Since virtually nothing is known about Norwegian bats, survey work is required to identify important roosts and feeding habitats.

Bibliography

* Solheim, R. (1987) *Fauna* 40, 83 -86.

6
Sweden

Especially over the last ten years, several research projects have developed to study the ecology, behaviour and conservation of bats. Much of this work has been done by professional scientists, but amateur groups are working in a number of areas. As a result, knowledge about the status and distribution of Swedish bat species increases rapidly.

Bat studies with ultrasonic detection started in 1978 and this technique has now provided detailed information on distribution and abundance of bats in a number of provinces in central and southern Sweden.

About 2,000 localities were surveyed and several thousand kilometres of line transects on roads have been completed, by driving at night with a microphone mounted on a car. Little work has been done elsewhere and knowledge about the distribution and status of the bat fauna is still very incomplete. Sixteen species of bat have been recorded and eleven species are known to breed. It is likely another three species have nursery colonies, while two species are thought to be occasional vagrants.

Observations suggest that four or five species may be increasing, four are decreasing, while the remaining established species do not show significant local change.

Feeding Habits

Sheltered, luxuriant, deciduous woodland, bordering streams is prime feeding habitat used by a number of species, especially *M. nattereri*, *M. daubentonii* and *M. dasycneme*. The latter two also

Swedish Bats and their Status

Scientific & Local Name	Frequency of Occurrence	Status
Myotis mystacinus (Mustaschfladdermus)	Common occurring to 62°N	Nt
Myotis brandtii (Brandts fladdermus)	Common occurring to 64°N	Nt
Myotis daubentonii (Vattenfladdermus)	Common widespread species near woodland and fresh or even marine water bodies	Nt
Myotis dasycneme (Dammfladdermus)	Very rare, occurring in two regions but only one known colony in south	R
Myotis nattereri (Fransfladdermus)	Probably rare but widespread north to central Sweden	CD
Myotis bechsteinii (Bechsteins fladdermus)	Very rare. Only found in southernmost province	E
Myotis myotis (Stort Musöra)	Only one record	--
Pipistrellus pipistrellus (Dvärgfladdermus)	Common in southern areas, rare and restricted habitats further north	Nt
Pipistrellus nathusii (Trollfladdermus)	Recently discovered in scattered localities, north to central Sweden	R
Eptesicus serotinus (Syfladdermus)	Very rare. First found in 1982 in south	R
Eptesicus nilssonii (Nordisk fladdermus)	Very common. Often only species found in coniferous forest. Most abundant species in Sweden	Nt
Vespertilio murinus (Graskimlig fladdermus)	Common in south and central areas, probably spreading north	Nt
Nyctalus noctula (Stor fladdermus)	Common over flat country in south and central Sweden. Rare elsewhere	CD
Plecotus auritus (Langörad fladdermus)	Common in southern Sweden	Nt
Plecotus austriacus (Gra langörad fladdermus)	Possible vagrant. Two specimens reported in 1960s	--
Barbastella barbastellus (Barbastell)	Rare, but observed regularly up to 58°N	V

Note: *M. dasycneme* is classed as endangered in north west Europe as a whole.   C D: care demanding specialise in feeding over the water and *M. daubentonii* is also known to exploit food over sheltered marine waters. Within forests, *M. brandtii* and *M. mystacinus* feed along rides and in glades, while *M. bechsteinii* and *P. auritus* feed amongst the trees, but mostly in deciduous or mixed forest areas.

Urban habitats are utilised primarily by *P. pipistrellus, E. nilssonii* and *V. murinus.*

Only one species, *E. nilssonii,* is common and widespread in the major areas of conifer forest, but it has shown a recent tendency to spread into urban areas.

Roosts

Summer Roosts

Hollow trees form a major roost resource for most species. They are especially important for *M. bechsteinii, M. dasycneme, M. brandtii, M. mystacinus, N. noctula* and *P. auritus.*

House roofs and walls are occupied occasionally by almost all species, but nurseries are found there of *M. dasycneme, M. brandtii, M. mystacinus, M. nattereri, V. murinus, E. nilssonii* and *P. pipistrellus.*

N. nattereri often roosts in vaulted stonework, especially in old bridges, cellars or watermills. A significant number of *P. auritus* colonies are found in churches.

Winter Roosts

All kinds of sites are used for hibernation, from buildings to hollow trees. Caves, mines, cellars and tunnels are used in addition to those used in summer.

Threats

It is probable most species suffered as a result of habitat changes earlier this century. At that time permanent meadows, once used for haymaking, were cultivated for crops and an important bat food source disappeared. Canalisation of water courses, renovation of buildings and cutting down of hollow trees all result in the reduction of feeding areas and roost sites.

Swedish forest law states that hollow trees should not be felled, but this obligation is not always obeyed.

Renovation of old buildings such as castles and fortifications reduces roosts by blocking access to them and it may also kill bats by blocking entrances when bats are inside. *M. nattereri* is threatened by the renovation of watermills, and construction of mini hydro-electric power stations within them. Also, disturbance of roosts sometimes causes bats to move, perhaps to poorer sites where survival is reduced.

The Swedish bat fauna is probably suffering from pollution. Small numbers of *P. pipistrellus* and *M. daubentonii* from the province of Skane were analysed for pesticides and showed low levels of organochlorine residues (DDE and PCB). Even small amounts of stored DDE can increase the metabolic rate of bats and at a time when food is sparse, vital food reserves will be utilised and some animals may starve. Bats at high latitudes have to face a more severe climate and a longer period of hibernation than those living further south, therefore survival may be reduced by low levels of pesticides.

However, some recent severe winters have affected bats in Skane, more than others further north in central Sweden.

Key Sites

A series of hibernacula are important for a variety of species and a few of these have some measure of protection.

Disused mines used for hibernation are already protected with grilles, for example Eriksdal, in the Province of Skane; another at Taberg in Smaland, and the cave of Lummelunda in the Province of Gotland. The lime pit area, Ignaberga, and the lime pit/cave, Balsberg, both in Skane, are also protected with grilles.

Three other important mines -- Gladsax, Province of Skane; mine of Kleva; Vetlanda in Smaland and at Herräng in Uppland are unprotected at present. These underground sites are used by the cavernicolous species including the *Myotis*, except *M. dasycneme* (but including *E. nilssonii*). The sites at Gladsax and Balsberg are especially valuable for *B. barbastellus* and Ignaberga for the endangered *M. bechsteinii*.

Two other mines contain the largest known Swedish populations in hibernation. At Dannemora, Province of Uppland, *E. nilssonii, M. daubentonii, M. nattereri* and *P. auritus*, total a few hundred specimens, and are not accessible to the public. The silver mine of Sala, Västmanland, gives some protection to perhaps up to one thousand bats of the same species.

Large old buildings are especially vital for some bat populations in hibernation. Fort of Varberg, Province of Halland, has a population of *B. barbastellus* and *P. auritus* protected by grilling, and the fortress near Waxholm (Uppland) shelters a number of species including *M. nattereri* and the endangered *M. dasycneme*. The fortification of Karlsborg (Västergötland) has a significant population of *B. barbastellus* and *P. auritus*, which are not accessible to the public.

Additionally, the only known nursery of *M. dasycneme* occurs in an uninhabited house in the municipality of Skurup (Skane). These bats also roost in a hollow tree. Protection will be needed for all roosts of this species, which is now being found over a wider area.

Protected Sites

Although a number of sites have been protected with grilles, there is need for more to be done. There is a need to safeguard all important roosts with legal protection as well as physical barriers as appropriate.

Creation of New Roosts

One of the research projects tested different designs of bat boxes. Comparisons were made between different types and it was possible to evaluate the best ones for the different bat species. Boxes made of sawdust/concrete or porous concrete, were superior to those made of wood in attracting bats. The main reason seemed to be that boxes made of concrete remained drier inside.

Conservation of Endangered Species

A conservation strategy is needed for the endangered *M. bechsteinii*. Only one hibernacula has been protected (Ignaberga lime pits area) and little is known about what elements of habitat are vital for its conservation. Likewise, the European endangered species *M. dasycneme* requires a carefully devised strategy of research, protection and management, with continued cooperation between the key countries of Denmark and the Netherlands.

Legislation

One of the most important achievements of the bat project was to gain full legal protection for bats. Swedish bats were fully protected by law in 1986; their roosts however, are generally not protected. Nor is there any obligation to search for bats in houses which are to be treated with harmful pesticide. New legislation is needed to cover these vital aspects.

Education

An important aspect of the conservation programme, has been publicity through the media. Most of the daily newspapers have carried articles about bats, their ecology and the bat projects. There is a need for education materials for all parts of society and especially for schools.

Research

More detailed knowledge is needed on the habitats used by the different species, in order to establish which resources are critical. This is a prerequisite before wider conservation programmes can be considered.

Pesticides in the general environment are probably affecting bats, but we do not know at which contamination levels the bats will be affected by them.

Bibliography

- Ahlén, I. (1981) Identification of Scandinavian bats by their sound. *Swedish Univ. Agric. Sci.* Rep. 6, 1-56.

- Ahlén, I. & Gerell, R. (1987) Distribution and status of bats in Sweden. *Proc. 4th EBRC 1987.*

- Gerell, R. (1985) Tests for boxes for bats. *Nyctalus* (N.F.) 2, 181-185.

7
Finland

A number of bat studies have been conducted in Finland since the 1960s, but overall the bat fauna is poorly recorded. However, in recent years wider interest has developed following several articles published in the popular press. This has resulted in ornithologists and other people reporting observations to Dr. T. Stjernberg, Zoological Museum, University of Helsinki, Norra Jarnvagagatan 13, SF-00100, Helsingfors, Finland.

Five species of bat are known to breed in Finland, *Myotis mystacinus, M. brandtii, M. daubentonii, Eptesicus nilssonii* and *Plecotus auritus*. Also several other species are found in the summer, and may have nurseries. No sites have been specifically protected for bats, despite protection being given to the animals in 1923.

Roosts

Summer Roosts

Relatively few nursery roosts have been identified, but *M. mystacinus* and *M. brandtii* appear only to use trees. *M. daubentonii* primarily frequent trees but also occupies bat boxes and buildings. *P. auritus* live in similar roosts, preferring buildings, while *E. nilssonii* almost exclusively use buildings.

Legislation and Conservation Measures

Finland was one of the first European States to enact legislation to protect bats. This was under the Nature Conservation Act (No

Finnish Bats and their Status

Scientific and Local Name	Frequency of Occurrence	Status
Myotis mystacinus (Viiksisiippa[1]) (Mindre mustaschfladdermus[2])	Common in southern half of country	Nt
Myotis brandtii (Isoviiksisiippa[1]) (Brandts mustaschfladdermus[2])	Very common north to central Finland	Nt
Myotis daubentonii (Vesisiippa[1]) (Vattenfladdermus[2])	Very common in southern areas	Nt
Myotis nattereri (Ripsisiippa[1]) (Fransfladdermus[2])	Probably a scattered population in central and southern Finland	V
Pipistrellus nathusii (Pikkulepakko[1]) (Trollfladdermus[2])	Two recent records in south	I
Eptesicus nilssonii (Pohjanlepakko[1]) (Nordisk fladdermus[2])	Common and widespread throughout	Nt
Vespertilio murinus (Kimolepakko[1]) (Graskimlig fladdermus[2])	No recent records; perhaps only a vagrant	--
Nyctalus noctula (Isolepakko[1]) (Stor fladdermus[2])	A few recent records in central and southern areas	R
Plecotus auritus (Korvayökkö[1]) (Langörad fladdermus[2])	Widespread in southern areas but possibly in low numbers	K

[1] = Finnish; [2] = Swedish. Both official languages of Finland.

71/1923), which was amended in April 1962 (No 292). The bats are protected, as well as their roosts when bats are present.

Education and Research

As a result of extensive publicity about bats, provided by the late Ruedi Lehmann and Finnish biologists, public opinion has changed, and bats are no longer regarded as creatures of superstition. There is a rapidly increasing interest and concern for bats, partly because of well publicised conservation projects such as trials using different types of bat boxes.

Much more research is needed before detailed conservation plans can be formulated. The basic questions requiring anwsers include: which species reproduce in Finland; what is the distribution of species; what kinds of roosts do they use in summer and for hibernation and what habitats are most important for each species? If adequate finance can be found, the present developing interest in bats should ensure some answers will soon be forthcoming.

8

Estonia SSR

Bat studies have developed steadily since the 1940s, carried out by both professionals and amateurs. Several hundred roost sites are documented and many are visited regularly to count the bats in summer and winter. Although there have been some large declines, other populations appear stable and some are increasing. Much of the work is conducted by M. Masing, Roomu tee 2, Institute of Forestry, Tartu, Estonia, 202400, USSR.

Eleven species are known to live and breed in Estonia. Two others may occur, *Barbastella barbastellus* and *Nyctalus leisleri*, since they are known in Latvia.

Roosts

Summer Roosts

All species use buildings for their nurseries, except *Myotis daubentonii*, *M. nattereri* and *Nyctalus noctula*, which are found mostly in trees. *M. dasycneme* requires large roof spaces near larger lakes and rivers, while *Plecotus auritus* exploits all types of roosts but tends to prefer buildings and trees.

All the Myotis species resort to caves in winter and large numbers of *P. auritus* and *Eptesicus nilssonii* hibernate in cellars. There are over 10,000 cellars in Estonia, some of which are very important for bats.

Bats of Estonia SSR and their Status

Scientific and Local Name	Frequency of Occurrence	Status
Myotis mystacinus (Habelendlane)	Found throughout but uncommon	R
Myotis brandtii (Brandti lendlane)	Fairly common but mostly in north west	Nt
Myotis daubentonii (Veelendlane)	Common and widespread	Nt
Myotis dasycneme (Tiigilendlane)	Mostly in north west coastal areas, rare elsewhere	V
Myotis nattereri (Nattereri lendlane)	Mainly occurs in central and western areas	R
Pipistrellus pipistrellus (Kääbus-nahkhiir)	Uncommon	I
Pipistrellus nathusii (Pargi-nahkhiir)	Common everywhere	Nt
Eptesicus nilssonii (Póhja-nahkhiir)	Very common throughout country	Nt
Vespertilio murinus (Suur-nahkhiir)	Uncommon	R
Nyctalus noctula (Suurvidevlane)	Uncommon	V
Plecotus auritus (Suurkórv)	Common throughout country	Nt

Threats

Three major problems concern hibernating bats. Firstly, open cast mining is destroying caves. Secondly, other caves are having their entrances blocked. Caves are a very limited resource in Estonia, therefore they have an intrinsic value in excess of the bat interest. The third problem is bats vacating roosts as a result of over-disturbance by people. At Humala, south west of Tallinn, three caves containing five species, showed a decline from 250 bats in the mid 1960s to about 70 bats in 1987. Similarly, another three caves further east at Laagri, sheltered 200 to 300 bats in the mid 1940s. Forty years later less than half over-winter there.

Small tunnel systems are too cold for bats in severe winters and because of this the number of caves and mines which are suitable for hibernation is limited.

Key Sites

A total of 16 caves is important for the hibernation of at least five, perhaps seven species of bat. Ten caves are near Tallinn on the north west coast; a single cave at Viti contains about 100 bats; three caves at Humala are used by approximately 70 bats; Vääna-Posti has two caves with numbers of bats totalling about 500; Laagri's three caves have about 100 bats and a cave at Ülgase shelters about 200 bats. In the extreme south east of the State, six caves around Piusa totalled 800 hibernating bats in 1978. Bats in this area have shown a remarkable increase from only about 20 bats in the late 1940s to 400 in the mid 1970s.

Five key areas to summer habitat have been identified, showing a combination of good feeding habitat, abundant roost sites and a wide variety of bats. One site, Alatskivi, east of Tartu, near lake Peipus, has at least eight species. The other sites in central southern and south west Estonia, are Limnoloogia, Pilasilla Vóiste and Kabli. The latter, close to the Latvian border, appears to be on a migration route for bats, especially *Pipistrellus nathusii.* One specimen of this species was recovered 1490 kilometres south west. Ten species have been found in the area in late summer.

Protected Sites

Parts of the caves in Piusa were given protection in 1981. All the other key cave sites need protection.

Creation of New Roost Sites

There is great scope for the development of a network of hiber-nacula across Estonia. With minimal expense, the huge number of cellars could be converted to provide environmental conditions suitable for bats. Some isolated sites will need grilling, or other artificial barriers, to prevent unauthorised access.

Legislation and Conservation Measures

Although bats were protected in 1958, roost site protection is in-adquate. Special areas should be created as protected conservation sites and suitable legislation is needed to effect this.

Education and Research

There has been little implementation of the legislation. Information needs to be widely circulated to explain the principles of bat conservation. There is a need to coordinate research projects and seek the cooperation of research workers, to help with conservation projects. A coordinated approach of surveys for summer and winter sites, is also being sought.

Bibliography

Masing M. (1984) *Lendlased.* Tallinn, Valgus.

9
Latvia SSR

A full report was not received.

Thirteen bat species are known, and twelve have been included in the Latvian Red Data Book. A recent single specimen of *Nyctalus leisleri* was found near the Baltic coast, but it is not known whether this was a vagrant.

One of the bat specialists is: Mrs.I. Busa, Oktobra Street 12, Jurmala 11, Latvia 229 081, USSR.

A number of important bat roosts are protected because they occur in nature reserves.

All bats were given protection in April 1957, and this was enhanced in 1977 with Regulation no. 241 (ref.: 5) Supplement no. 14 of the Council of Ministries. Bat roosts are not specially protected under this legislation.

Conservation needs will be similar to those of Estonia SSR.

Bats of Latvia SSR and their Status

Scientific and Local Name	Frequency of Occurrence	Status
Myotis mystacinus	Very rare	V
Myotis brandtii	Uncommon, few records from north and west	V
Myotis daubentonii	Common	Nt
Myotis dasycneme	Uncommon, but mostly in east	V
Myotis nattereri	Rare, found in north and west	V
Pipistrellus pipistrellus	Rare	V
Pipistrellus nathusii	Common, widespread	Nt
Eptesicus nilssonii	Very common everywhere	Nt
Vespertilio murinus	Rare, few records	V
Nyctalus noctula	Fairly common everywhere	V
Nyctalus leisleri	Single record	K
Plecotus auritus	Common everywhere	V
Barbastella barbastellus	Rare	V

10
Lithuania

No report was received. There is no known bat specialist.

Although no bats are listed in the Red Data Book, a few bat sites have been specially protected with grilles to prevent disturbance by people. The species list is similar to Latvia. No *Nyctalus leisleri* has been found, but a few *Eptesicus serotinus* occur in the south.

Conservation needs will be similar to Estonia SSR.

Kaliningrad Oblast

This small territory, lying between Lithuania and Poland, is an isolated part of the Russian SFSR. There is no known bat specialist. Bat roosts are not specially protected.

11
Poland

Poland appears to form an important link between the bat populations in Scandinavia, Finland, and the Baltic Soviet Socialist Republics and those in countries further south in central and southern Europe. Bats are known to migrate between these areas and successful conservation will depend upon measures being taken over a wide area.

Poland is also especially important because it has the largest population of bats hibernating in one site of anywhere in Europe. This site is the Nietoperek tunnels west of Poznan.

For many years only a small number of biologists were interested in bats, but in 1987 a major initiative was taken with the founding of the Chiropterological Information Centre (CIC). The aim of this project is to gather and exchange information on bats, survey and catalogue bat roosts and coordinate research and bat ringing.

There have been regular surveys of important hibernacula and results show *Rhinolophus hipposideros* has declined almost to extinction in 35 years.

Also a very large colony of 3,000 *Myotis myotis*, living in the Kraków, St Maria Church in the 1950s, declined and disappeared for no known reason. However, though *M. myotis* populations in Lower Silesia declined in the late 1960s and early 1970s by 11 per cent per year, their numbers have increased again by an average of 5 per cent per year, over the past 15 years; which means there are now 84 per cent of the number in the late 1960s.

Polish Bats and their Status

Scientific and Local Name	Frequency of Occurrence	Status
Rhinolophus ferrumequinum (Podkowiec duzy)	Vagrant. One record	--
Rhinolophus hipposideros (Podkowiec maly)	Rare, found in south of country, under rapid decline	E(E)
Myotis mystacinus (Nocek wasatek)	Fairly rare. Widespread and more abundant in south	V
Myotis brandtii (Nocek Brandta)	Fairly rare. Widespread and more abundant in south	V
Myotis emarginatus (Nocek orzesiony)	Very rare, close to extinction in central and southern areas	E
Myotis daubentonii (Nocek rudy)	Very common throughout	Nt
Myotis dasycneme (Nocek lydkowlosy)	Rare. Scattered records throughout	I^2
Myotis nattereri (Nocek natterera)	Common throughout	V
Myotis bechsteinii (Nocek Bechsteina)	Very rare. Mostly in south and west	I(V)
Myotis myotis (Nocek duzy)	Fairly common in central and southern areas	V
Pipistrellus pipistrellus (Karlik malutki)	Fairly common throughout	I
Pipistrellus nathusii (Karlik wiekszy)	Rare. Scattered records throughout	I
Eptesicus serotinus (Mroczek pózny)	Very common throughout	Nt
Eptesicus nilssonii (Mroczek pozlocisty)	Rare. Small numbers found occasionally in east and in mountains	I(R)
Vespertilio murinus (Mroczek posrebrzany)	Rare. Mostly in central and eastern areas	I(R)

Polish Bats and their Status (continued)

Scientific and Local Name	Frequency of Occurrence	Status
Nyctalus noctula (Borowiec wielki)	Common and widespread	Nt
Nyctalus leisleri (Borowiaczek)	Very rare. Scattered records in east, south and west central areas	I(R)
Nyctalus Iasiopterus (Borowiec olbrzymi)	Vagrant. One record in central Poland	--
Plecotus auritus (Gacek brunatny)	Very common	Nt
Plecotus austriacus (Gacek szary)	Fairly common in central and southern areas	I
Barbastella barbastellus (Mopek)	Fairly common in central and southern areas	V

[1] - Polish Red Data Book in brackets ( );
[2] - European endangered species

Nevertheless, many bat populations are in decline and one of the important tasks of the CIC is to monitor and coordinate observations.

Feeding Habitats

Substantial degradation of feeding habitat in the Sudety Mountain regions of Lower Silesia, caused by 'acid rain', appears to be the reason for substantial bat declines in that area. Forestry policy favours replanting previously deciduous woodlands with conifers, and changes in insect variety and abundance can be expected.

Roosts

Summer Roosts

All resident breeding species are known to roost in buildings, especially in summer. Some nurseries of *R. hipposideros* used to occur in caves but none now remain; one possible explanation is a gradual reduction in cave temperature which reflects a slight lowering of annual temperature in that area. High roost temperatures are essential for successful breeding, particularly for bats with a small body mass.

Winter Roosts

Bats use all kinds of sites for hibernation, particularly buildings, hollow trees, fortifications and caves. Sites which give adequate protection are especially important because of the regular periods of extreme cold weather in north east Europe. Such places are in relatively short supply in areas to the north and east of Poland, and bats will migrate long distances to take advantage of sheltered roosts. The extensive area of the Kraków to Wielun Upland, a limestone plateau, contains a large number of caves and collectively, these make up one of the most important bat hibernacula areas of northern Europe.

Threats

Loss of forests due to 'acid rain' in the Lower Silesian area (Sudety Mountains) appears to have affected the bat populations. Felling of deciduous forests containing many hollow trees and replacing with conifer plantations, is reducing roosts and food.

Modern building methods and architectural styles do not create sites suitable for many species, whilst renovation of old buildings is excluding long established colonies. Blocking of under-roof spaces in churches to exclude nesting birds, but which also excludes bats; together with the continuing direct killing of bats which are causing a 'nuisance'.

Utilisation of old fortifications is a major threat. So too is the destruction of some fortifications regarded as dangerous, such as parts of the Modlin fortress.

Most important by far is the proposal to dump spent radioactive materials in the former defence tunnels near Miedzyrzecz, about 50 kilometres west of Pozhan.

Especially important is the development of tourism in caves in the limestone Karst areas, which is disturbing bats and preventing them from hibernating in traditional sites. The close proximity to

Karst of the large human population around Katowice, has resulted in protective grilles on caves being quickly destroyed.

A significant problem has been the collection of bats for research.

Additional threats and causes of declines include the significant loss of the large cockchafer beetles (*Melolontha*), due to agricultural changes incorporating the extensive use of chemicals.

Key Sites

Miedzyrzecz tunnels are known to contain 20,000 bats of eleven species each winter, and a small breeding colony of *M. myotis* is found in the summer.

In winter there are about 12,000 *M. daubentonii*, 5,000 *M. myotis*, 300 *M. nattereri*, 1,000 *B. barbastellus*, 700 *P. auritus* and relatively small numbers of *M. mystacinus, M. brandtii, M. bechsteinii, M. dasycneme, E. serotinus* and *P. pipistrellus.* The 30 kilometres of artificial tunnels contain more than four times as many bats as any other known site in northern Europe and because bats gather there from surrounding states, it is of great international importance. There is a clear need to protect the entire system as a European Heritage site.

Other important fortifications are in Poznan and forts around Modlin near Warsaw, all used primarily for hibernation.

The Kraków to Wielun Upland has a number of caves of special significance to bats: Jaskinia Ciemna, Jaskinia Nietoperzowa, Jaskinia Raclawicka, Jaskinia Studnisko, Jaskinia Wierzchowska Gorna and Jaskinia Koralowa. Another cave crucial to the conservation of bats in this area, lies on the north west of the area near Wielun. This is Jaskinia Szachownica and houses the second largest population of hibernating bats in Poland. The site has been studied from 1981 to 1987 and shows a feature common to many caves, which is that counts of the numbers of bats present in March are, on average, double those made in late January. To a large extent this is caused by bats awakening to seek more sheltered and warmer roosts in periods of intense cold. On 7 March 1987, the largest number was recorded (1,477 bats): 374 *M. myotis*, 721 *M. nattereri*, 67 *M. mystacinus/brandtii*, 212 *M. daubentonii*, 80 *P. auritus* and a small number of at least two other species.

There are a series of mines in the Sudetes of Lower Silesia, especially in Glucholazy in the East Sudetes and Sowia Dolina in the Karkonosze, as well as Kamieniec Zabkowicki. These collectively shelter a large number of bats of a wide range of species. A school at Sokole Pole near Kraków, has a large breeding colony of *M. myotis*.

In addition to the above sites, over 150 other important localities are known in Poland.

Protected Sites

Only four sites have any protection. Part of the Miedzyrzecz fortification tunnels have been made into a bat nature reserve known as 'Nietoperek', but less than one quarter of the whole system is protected. Unfortunately, not only are some parts threatened by the proposal to use them as a nuclear waste dump, but because tunnels are open, tourists frequently disturb the hibernating bats.

It is vital for this entire system to be declared a fully protected area, with gates and adequate wardening.

Szachownica Cave near Wielun and Jaskinia Ciemna, situated in Ojcow National Park, are protected as natural reserves but not specifically for bats. The only other bat reserve is a municipal school building, Sokole Pole near Kraków, with a summer colony of *M. myotis*.

Conservation of Endangered Species

R. hipposideros is critically endangered in Poland and a programme for its conservation is required. All nursery sites should be given protection together with all significant roosts used for hibernation.

It may be too late to save *M. emarginatus* in Poland, as no nurseries are known and the species is rarely encountered. However, methodical searching ought to continue and sites, if found, should be protected.

The conservation of populations at the edge of a species range is equally as important as protecting the optimum or core areas.

Legislation

Under the Nature Conservation Act of 7 April 1949, bats, not being game animals, received protection. The protection was strengthened by the Ordinance of the Minister of Forestry and Wood Industry on 17 November 1952 and the Decree by the same minister, dated 30 December 1983. However, the legislation does not mention bats in particular and because of the peculiar and special roosting habits of these animals, their unique needs ought to receive legislative recognition. In particular, nursery and other key roosts should be protected by statute.

Implementation of existing legislation has been lacking, and is urgently needed. At present it is not an offence to disturb bats and there is no formal licensing of those wishing to do research on bats.

Education

Few people in Poland are aware of the fact that bats are protected and in need of conservation. While there has been a small number of professional biologists doing research, few other people have been aware of bats. The setting up of the Chiropterological Information Centre in 1987 (Dr B W Woloszyn, CIC, Institute of Systematic and Experimental Zoology, Polish Academy of Sciences, 31-016 Kraków, Poland), is an important step towards the coordination of research and dissemination of information. There is an urgent need to produce popular publications about bats and to use all parts of the media to educate all elements of society to the need to consider and conserve Poland's bat population. Clearly, some bats migrate internationally and this fact is a strong argument for help to be provided from outside Poland if required.

Research

Perhaps the foremost task is to establish an adequate trained network of people throughout the country, who can carefully undertake surveys of known sites and search for new ones. Generally scientists in universities lack some of the new equipment, such as bat detectors, which aid non-disturbance surveys during the summer.

12
Czechoslovakia

An extensive research programme has been conducted since the late 1940s. All kinds of topics were studied, from reproductive physiology, population ecology, migrations and systematics to the examination of sub-fossil bat records from cave deposits.

One of the themes followed for forty years was a ringing programme, to find whether seasonal movements or migration occurred and what the population densities were for each species in different habitats. Over 65,000 bats of 19 species were ringed from 1948 to 1987. Until 1967, bat ringing was carried out at almost every opportunity. At that time it was recognised that some ringing caused damage to populations being studied and because of the need to protect bats a modified programme was developed. This allows bat ringing only when clearly defined questions are being addressed. One of the co-ordinators for these studies is: Dr V Hanák, Institute of Systemic Zoology, Charles University, Vinicna 7, 128 44, Praha 2.

Bats were protected in 1965, but despite the interest in these creatures by a relatively large number of scientists, little information has reached the public on bat conservation. Overall most bat populations showed large declines in the 38 years to 1985, but recently many have stabilised. Numbers of *Myotis daubentonii* especially have increased in line with a similar growth in other European countries.

Despite the large bat ringing programme, movements are poorly understood. The usually migratory *Nyctalus noctula* appears to be comparatively sedentary in Czechoslovakia but long distance movements have been recorded for some species, including *N.*

Czechoslovakian Bats and their Status

Scientific and Local Name	Frequency of Occurrence	Status
Rhinolophus ferrumequinum (Vrápenec velky)[1] (Podkovár vel'ky)[2]	Occurs mostly in south and east, rare elsewhere	E
Rhinolophus hipposideros (Vrápenec maly)[1] (Podkovár maly)[2]	Found throughout, most frequent in southeast	E
Rhinolophus euryale (Vrápenec jizní)[1] (Podkovár juzny)[2]	Very rare in southeast	E*
Myotis mystacinus (Netopyr vousaty)[1] (Netopier fúzaty)[2]	Common throughout	V
Myotis brandtii (Netopyr Brandtuv)[1] Netopier Brandtov)[2]	Widespread in low numbers	V
Myotis emarginatus (Netopyr brvity)[1] Netopier brvity)[2]	Rare, mainly in southeast	V
Myotis daubentonii (Netopyr vodní)[1] (Netopier vodny)[2]	Common in west and south	Nt
Myotis dasycneme (Netopyr pobrezní)[1] (Netopier pobrezny)[2]	Uncommon everywhere	E
Myotis nattereri (Netopyr rasnaty)[1] (Netopier riasnaty)[2]	Common throughout country	V
Myotis bechsteinii (Netopyr velkouchy)[1] Netopier vel'kouchy)[2]	Very rare everywhere	R
Myotis myotis (Netopyr velky)[1] Netopier obycajny)[2]	Found throughout	V
Myotis blythi (Netopyr vychodní)[1] (Netopier vychodny)[2]	Occurs in south and east, few records elsewhere	V

Czechoslovakian Bats and their Status (continued)

Scientific and Local Name	Frequency of Occurrence	Status
Pipistrellus pipistrellus (Netopyr hvízdavy)[1] (Vecernica malá)[2]	Common everywhere	V
Pipistrellus nathusii (Netopyr parkovy)[1] Vecernica parková)[2]	Low numbers everywhere, mostly in summer, migratory	R
Eptesicus serotinus (Netopyr vecerní)[1] (Vecernica pozdna)[2]	Common everywhere except mountains	V
Eptesicus nilssonii (Netopyr severní)[1] (Vecernica severská)[2]	Common everywhere mostly in mountains	V
Vespertilio murinus (Netopyr pestry)[1] (Vecernica tmavá)[2]	Rare over entire country	R
Nyctalus noctula (Netopyr rezavy)[1] (Raniak hrdzavy)[2]	Fairly common throughout country	V
Nyctalus leisleri (Netopyr stromovy)[1] (Raniak maly)[2]	Occurs throughout country in low numbers	R
Nyctalus lasiopterus (Netopyr obrovsky)[1] (Raniak velky)[2]	A rare vagrant	R*
Miniopterus schreibersi (Létavec stenhovavy)[1] (Lietavec st'ahovavy)[2]	Rare in extreme south, migratory	E*
Plecotus auritus (Netopyr usaty)[1] (Uchác svetly)[2]	Common everywhere except tree-less south east	V
Plecotus austriacus (Netopyr dlouhouchy)[1] (Uchác sivy)[2]	Found everywhere, common in lowlands	V
Barbastella barbastellus (Netopyr cerny)[1] (Uchana cierna)[2]	Found everywhere but less common in east	V

[1] Czech name; [2] Slovak name -- both official languages
* Very rare occurrence in Czechoslovakia

leisleri, Pipistrellus pipistrellus and *M. brandtii*. One specimen of the latter was recovered, having been ringed in Lithuania.

Threats

Changes in landscape are thought to have been particularly damaging to bats. Extensive removal of woods and shelter belts with the concomitant loss of tree roosts and insects, has been especially significant for bats. The National campaign to renovate old and historic buildings is inadvertently both killing bats, and depriving them of roosts. There has been a tremendous increase in recreational caving which disturbs bats and drives them away, also some bats are being killed by vandals.

*Plate 10. The lesser horseshoe bat, **Rhinolophus hipposideros**, is already extinct in some areas. Often the causes are unknown, but this tiny six gramme bat appears to be particularly sensitive to changes in climate and environment.*

Protected Sites

There are many caves and mines which are important for hibernation. These, and other bat roosts are protected by law but some are specifically protected as reserves: In Bohemia, the mines Herlíkovické stoly of the south east; habitat at Bouda in the north east; natural monument 'Tynec' in the south west and the State nature reserve in Slovakia including mines, Dubnické bane in the south east. Hibernation sites in some limestone caves received specific protection, for example, Bycí skála, Moravsky kras-stred, Turold and Spranek. Caves are also specially protected in the national parks, Pieniny and Low Tatra Mountains in central Slovakia, the protected landscape areas of the Czech karst in central Bohemia, Moravian karst (in the south) and the southern Slovak karst.

Legislation

Bats were protected in 1965, both in the Czech Socialist Republic, (Ministry of Culture No 80) and the Slovak Socialist Republic, (Slovak National Council No 125). Roosts are also given protection when bats are in residence, but there is a need to give roosts special protection at all times. A change in the legislation is required to achieve this.

Education

Some leaflets and booklets have been produced explaining the importance of particular sites to bats. However, leaflets have not received the wide circulation to the public which is necessary to give detailed information about the importance of bat conservation. Continued vandalism of caves and bats is probably largely a result of ignorance.

Research

Scientists in Czechoslovakia are amongst the leaders in European bat research, but their work is hampered by the lack of bat detectors for field work and computers for processing their extensive results. Regular annual monitoring of hibernacula has been conducted for many years and will form part of the core for wider European co-operation.

Bibliography

- Gaisler, J. and Bauerova, Z. (1986) The life of bats in a city. *Myotis*. 23-24, 209-215.

- Gaisler, J. and Hanák. V. (1969) Ergebnisse der Zwanzigjahrigen Beringung von Fledermusen (Chiroptera) in der Tschechoslowakei: 1948-1967. *Acta Sci. nat. Acad. Sci. bohemslov*. Brno, 3, 1-33.

- Horácek, J. and Hanák, V. (1986) Generic status of *Pipistrellus savii* and comments on classification of the genus *Pipistrellus* (Chiroptera, Vespertilionidae). *Myotis*. 23-24, 9-16.

13

Democratic Republic of Germany

Bats in Germany were originally given protection in 1936. This reflected the detailed knowledge of the time, from research which began in the late 1920s and continues today. The pioneer studies of Martin Eisentraut, who examined the biology and natural history of bats throughout northern Germany, served to inspire others throughout Europe and North America. His detailed experiments showed some bats made extensive seasonal movements and others were capable of homing from distances in excess of 100 kilometres. Some of the bats ringed by Eisentraut were recaptured in other countries.

From the late 1940s, detailed ecological research and roost monitoring continued. These activities, including ringing, are co-ordinated at the Institut für Landschaftsforschung und Natursshutz, Stübelallee 2, 8019 Dresden.

Threats

Replacement of deciduous trees with conifers, is reducing the number of roost sites and variety of insects. Much of the felling of old broad-leaved forest occurs in the summer, killing juvenile bats as well as depriving them of roosts. In 1984 and 1985, DDT was used against the night flying moth *Lymantria monacha*. This, together with other chemicals used in forestry and agriculture, is believed to have contributed to bat deaths. Loss of hedgerow trees, copses and ponds in agricultural areas is considered to be causing observed reductions in bat populations, as well other threats including killing, and excluding bats from roof spaces, walls, tombs and other sites.

Bats of the Democratic Republic of Germany and their Status

Scientific and Local Name	Frequency of Occurrence	Status
Rhinolophus hipposideros (Kleine Hufeisennase)	Small number in south and south west	E[1]
Myotis mystacinus (Kleine Bartfledermaus)	Small number found throughout	E
Myotis brandtii (Grosse Bartfledermaus)	Low density throughout	R
Myotis daubentonii (Wasserfledermaus)	Common everywhere	V
Myotis dasycneme (Teichfledermaus)	Small numbers found occasionally	R
Myotis nattereri (Fransenfledermaus)	Common	V
Myotis bechsteinii (Bechsteinfledermaus)	Widely distributed but rare	R
Myotis myotis (Mausohr)	Very rare, found mostly in south	E[1]
Pipistrellus pipistrellus (Zwergfledermaus)	Common, occurs throughout country	V
Pipistrellus nathusii (Rauhhautfledermaus)	Low numbers throughout	V
Eptesicus serotinus (Breitflügelfledermaus)	Common everywhere	V
Eptesicus nilssonii (Nordfledermaus)	Small numbers mostly in east	V
Vespertilio murinus (Zweifarbfledermaus)	Rare, mostly in east	R
Nyctalus noctula (Abendsegler)	Occurs everywhere	V
Nyctalus leisleri (Kleiner Abendsegler)	A few records from southern part of country	R

Bats of the Democratic Republic of Germany and their Status (continued)

Scientific and Local Name	Frequency of Occurrence	Status
Plecotus auritus (Braunes Langohr)	Common everywhere	V
Plecotus austriacus (Graues Langohr)	Common in southern half of country	V
Barbastella barbastellus (Mopsfledermaus)	Throughout	E

1 This species is critically endangered

Key Sites

There is a need to protect all roosts and feeding habitat of *Myotis myotis* and *Rhinolophus hipposideros*. For the former special protection is difficult due to the large area used by the bats, but for the more sedentary *R. hipposideros* site protection is more practical in the region of Thüringen, Saale-Unstrut-Gebiet and from Dresden southwards. The Rüdersdorf near Berlin, is a major hibernaculum which contains about 2,000 bats, mostly *M. daubentonii*. This requires protection.

Legislation

Bats were protected in 1970 and the statute was reinforced from October 1984. In the latest amendments to the legislation, species are given different levels of protection according to their status, together with protection for all roosts, for example houses, trees and caves. Licences to disturb bats are required for research, photography and roost visiting.

Education

Although there is sympathetic media coverage of the need for bat protection and colour leaflets are being produced and circulated, there is still much to do to make conservation more effective. The public support conservation efforts, but official protection of roosts and habitat is necessary.

Research

Much of the seasonal monitoring of roosts conforms with the pattern being adopted within many European countries. Further cooperation between States will ensure co-ordination of conservation projects, especially for the endangered species.

Bibliography

- Hiebsches, H. (1983) Faunistische Kartierung der Fledermäuse in der DDR. *Nyctalus.* (NF), 1, 489-503.

- Schmidt, A. (1987) Möglichkeiten der Bestandserhaltung und Bestandshebung bei unseren Waldfledermäusen. *Beeskower nat. wiss.* Abh. 1, 28-36.

- Zöllick, H. and Hackethal, H. (1985) Zerstörtes Fledermausquartier in der Rostocker, Stadtmauer. *Nyctalus.* (NF), 2, 127-132.

14

Federal Republic of Germany

Much of our present knowledge about bats stems from a detailed research base provided by German scientists more than 50 years ago. This tradition of substantial research studies, is not only being maintained but is being extended into the conservation of bats, aided by a rapidly developing interest by amateurs. However, although bats are protected nationally, the individual States of the Federation (eleven authorities including West Berlin), have differing impetus in implementing protection. There are national and State Red Data lists of protected species, but because of the large size of the country (spanning over 800 kilometres north to south), there is a considerable variation in distribution and abundance of bats and in the status categories assigned to species.

Because of the Federal system, there is no single authority co-ordinating conservation and research. However, exchange of information especially concerning the distribution and status of bats, occurs through the journal 'Myotis', edited by Dr H Roer, Museum Alexander Koenig, Adenauerallee 150-164, D-5300, Bonn 1.

Within each of the States there is wide variation in the public awareness of bat conservation issues. Some regional authorities have promoted substantial conservation programmes, with the aid of scientists and amateurs, while in others little work has been attempted. Activities range from protection of caves and colonies in buildings, to creation of new hibernacula in road building schemes, and one colony of the endangered *Rhinolophus hipposideros* was successfully transplanted from a building, which was subsequently destroyed.

Bats of the Federal Republic of Germany and their Status

Scientific and Local Name	Frequency of Occurrence	Status
Rhinolophus ferrumequinum (Grosse Hufeisennase)	Occurs in south; becoming very rare	E
Rhinolophus hipposideros (Kleine Hufeisennase)	Rare, occurs mostly in south, declining	E
Myotis mystacinus (Kleine Bartfledermaus)	Fairly common throughout	V
Myotis brandtii (Grosse Bartfledermaus)	Rare throughout	V
Myotis emarginatus (Wimperfledermaus)	Southern areas rare, declining	E
Myotis daubentonii (Wasserfledermaus)	Common everywhere	Nt
Myotis dasycneme (Teichfledermaus)	Very rare, possibly only winter migrant	I
Myotis nattereri (Fransenfledermaus)	Rare or absent in north west, fairly common elsewhere	V
Myotis bechsteinii (Bechstein-Fledermaus)	Fairly rare, absent in north west	R
Myotis myotis (Mausohr)	Absent in north west; declining in northern areas	V
Pipistrellus pipistrellus (Zwergfledermaus)	Common everywhere	Nt
Pipistrellus nathusii (Rauhhautfledermaus)	Fairly rare everywhere	V
Pipistrellus savii (Alpenfledermaus)	Small numbers in extreme south	V
Eptesicus serotinus (Breitflügelfledermaus)	Fairly common everywhere	V

Bats of the Federal Republic of Germany and their Status (continued)

Scientific and Local Name	Frequency of Occurrence	Status
Eptesicus nilssonii (Nordfledermaus)	Uncommon, occurs in south and east	V
Vespertilio murinus (Zweitarbfledermaus)	Fairly rare, possibly mostly vagrant, except south east	V
Nyctalus noctula (Abendsegler)	Occurs everywere, becoming rare in some areas	V
Nyctalus leisleri (Kleiner Abendsegler)	Absent in north, rare in south	V
Miniopterus schreibersii (Langflugelfledermaus)	Sporadic occurrence, mainly a vagrant	K
Plecotus auritus (Braunes Langohr)	Common everywhere	V
Plecotus austriacus (Graues Langohr)	Absent in north, fairly common in south	V
Barbastella barbastellus (Mopsfledermaus)	Rare and declining everywhere	E

Threats

In the last 40 years extensive agriculture and forestry development has caused the damage and loss of many important habitats such as pasture, avenues of old hollow trees and ponds. Together with insecticides and other types of pollutants they have all helped in the observed declines of many bat species. The modernisation of old bridges together with replacement of others unsuitable for bats, have served to further reduce roosting sites. Pesticide treatment of timber has caused the death of many bats. Numerous cellars have been sealed or dried out making them unsuitable for bats. Defence bunkers and tunnels which are often used as bat roosts have been filled in, and frequently both hibernation and summer sites such as bat boxes have been over-disturbed by people. Badly designed bat boxes have attracted Martens (*Martes* spp.), which kill bats.

Plate 11. *The mouse-eared bat,* **Myotis myotis,** *Europe's largest, once common bat, used to be found in huge colonies of many thousands, but now is rare or extinct, especially in parts of northern countries. This specimen is the last one known in Great Britain. A male, born in 1972, was still alive in 1987.*

Key and Protected Sites

There is a large number of important bat roosts throughout the country, many of which need protection. Several other important roost sites also require protection, including many of the subterranean defence bunkers, ice cellars, caves and hollow trees. There are too many sites to list individually but as an illustration there are already 100 protected hibernation roosts in Baden-Württemberg with another 150 in Hessen.

Creation of New Roosts

An artificial hibernaculum was successfully created beneath a road near Berkenthin, Schlieswig-Holstein. Within a year *Plecotus auritus* and *Myotis daubentonii* were found roosting. In Bayarn, a building which housed one of the last known colonies of *R. hipposideros* was to be demolished. To save the colony, a nearby building was modified to accommodate the bats, including the installation of under-roost heating. The new facilities were successfully adopted.

These different kinds of projects illustrate what is needed to ensure successful bat conservation.

Conservation of Endangered Species

Four species are regarded as endangered, *R. ferrumequinum, R. hipposideros, M. emarginatus* and *Barbastella barbastellus*. Urgent work is needed to identify causes of declines in these species, with special emphasis on adequate protection of all nurseries and important hibernacula. As these species are similarly endangered in surrounding States, concerted action should be taken.

Legislation and Conservation Needs

All bats and their roosts were protected by the 'Bundesartenschutzverordnung' of August 1980. However, this is general legislation and to some extent open to interpretation. There is a need for more explicit legislation to give protection to house-roosting bats, the preservation of old trees and sites such as old bunkers. Feeding habitat has not been protected specifically for bats and these areas are vital, especially those surrounding the nurseries of the endangered species.

Education

The recent upsurge in concern for bats has been dramatic. About 150 people in the Baden-Württemberg region, are already helping with bat conservation. However, interest is patchy across the country and the development of other amateur bat groups is an urgent requirement. To this end, a training programme for bat workers is being augmented, in parallel with education materials such as audio-visual information packs, books and leaflets. As lack of finance is limiting the effectiveness of this important work, it would be expedient if there was national co-ordination in these kinds of projects.

Research

There are many and various on-going research projects and some are orientated at conservation problems. One such project (University of Kiel), is examining public knowledge and attitudes about bats, with the aim of more effectively targeting future education programmes throughout the country.

There is a need to improve the basic information on distribution and status of species and to find ways of monitoring success of conservation programmes. One method being developed uses bat detectors along line transects. This technique may be chosen for wide use across Europe as one of a series of procedures to gather quantitative information on status.

Bibliography

- Blab, J., Nowak, E., Trautmann, W. and Sukopp, H. eds. (1984) *Rote liste der gefährdeten Tiere und Pflanzen in der Bundesrupublik Deutschland.* Kilda, Greven.

- Jüdes, U. (1985) *Fledermäuse und ihr Schutz. Informationen und Materialien für die regionale Naturschutzarbeit.* Kiel.

- Richarz, K. (1986) *Wir tun was für unsere Fledermäuse.* S-Natur, München.

- Roer, H. (1987) Erste Erfahrungen mit einem permethrin-haltigen holzschutzmittel in einer wochenstube des Mausohrs. *Myotis myotis. Myotis.* 25, 105-111.

15

The Netherlands

Substantial bat research began in the 1930s, stimulated in part by the work of M. Eisentraut in Germany. Leo Bels led the work which was mostly carried out in the South Limburg Province. His aims were to answer questions concerning persistence in roosts, age to breeding, homing ability and what were the natural movements between roosts. He ringed a large number of bats including some of most Dutch species. When Bels left the country in the early 1950s, the work was already being continued by J.W. Sluiter and P.F. van Heerdt. It was these scientists who first alerted other bat biologists to the declines occurring in the populations they studied and suggested that their activities were one of the major causes. The ringing programme was stopped and subsequent observation showed some populations began to recover.

Since those times (late 1950s), the Dutch biologists, both amateur and professional, have continued to lead the need for bat conservation programmes and have carried out further important research, which currently mostly involves annual long-term monitoring of populations.

All conservation and research is co-ordinated by Mr P. Lina, Ministerie van Landbouw en Visserij, Bezuidenhoutseweg 73, Postbus 20401, 2500 EK's-Gravenhage.

Declines in many species have been severe. A nursery colony of *Rhinolophus ferrumequinum* in South Limburg was not seen after 1940.

Similarly, *R. hipposideros* used to be abundant in some areas in the 1950s, but none now remain. *Myotis emarginatus* and *M. myotis* with nursery colonies, were also numerous at that time,

Bats of the Netherlands and their Status

Scientific and Local Name	Frequency of Occurrence	Status
Rhinolophus ferrumequinum (Grote hoefijzerneus)	One colony to 1940, few records since	Ex
Rhinolophus hipposideros (Kleine hoefijzerneus)	Originally found in south east, last seen in 1983	Ex
Myotis mystacinus (Baardvleermuis)	Small numbers found everywhere	V
Myotis brandtii (Brandt's vleermuis)	Possibly widespread but only few records	V
Myotis emarginatus (Ingekorven vleermuis)	Very rare, occurs in south east	E
Myotis daubentonii (Watervleermuis)	Common everywhere	Nt
Myotis dasycneme (Meervleermuis)	Rare, declining, widespread in north	E
Myotis nattereri (Franjestaart)	Rare but widespread	K
Myotis bechsteinii (Langoorvleermuis)	Very rare, few recent records	R
Myotis myotis (Vale vleermuis)	Rare, a few remain in south	E
Pipistrellus pipistrellus (Dwergvleermuis)	Very common everywhere	Nt
Pipistrellus nathusii (Nathusius' dwergvleermuis)	Recently discovered, widespread, status uncertain	I
Eptesicus serotinus (Laatvlieger)	Very common throughout country	Nt
Vespertilio murinus (Tweekleurige vleermuis)	Rare vagrant	--
Nyctalus noctula (Rosse vleermuis)	Fairly common everywhere, but probably declining	K

Bats of the Netherlands and their Status

Scientific and Local Name	Frequency of Occurrence	Status
Nyctalus leisleri (Bosvleermuis)	Very rare. Two recent records	K
Plecotus auritus Gewone grootoorvleermuis)	Widespread but in decline	V
Plecotus austriacus (Grijze grootoorvleermuis)	Rare, few records in south	K
Barbastella barbastellus (Mopsvleermuis)	Very rare, only in south	R

---

but now both are very rare. *M. mystacinus/brandtii* have declined by 75 per cent.

To 1986, nine large nursery colonies of *M. dasycneme* had disappeared, leaving only seven known. Much of the loss was due to renovation of buildings, often involving remedial timber treatment. In churches similarly treated, a 65 per cent decline was recorded in *Plecotus* spp. (mostly *P. auritus*) from 1965 to 1977. The observed decline of South Limburg bats in hibernation, is 90 per cent in 40 years.

Threats

Some of the threats which formerly contributed to many of the large declines, have already been controlled. For example, disturbance of bats in hibernacula is now controlled by grilles, and strict licensing of research activities. However, landscape changes, especially involving loss of old trees and woodland, are having an adverse affect on bats. Linear habitats, especially shelter belts of trees, are important flight-ways for bats and fragmentation of these appears to be disturbing established patterns of bat movements.

Key and Protected Sites

Since 1980 more than 40 limestone mines in South Limburg Province have been protected with grilles. Others are planned. The vitally important St Pietersberg mines, already partially destroyed by a local cement manufacturing industry's quarrying, require total protection. These tunnels are of immense historic value due to their antiquity and occupation by European peoples over many centuries.

Military defence tunnels and bunkers are being protected as hibernacula, particularly in the North Sea coastal dune areas and near Arnhem, as are some government owned old fortresses.

Creation of New Sites

Five artificial tunnels for hibernation have been constructed and others are planned. Perhaps more important, two limestone mine systems have been reopened in South Limburg.

Conservation of Endangered Species

Two endangered species *Myotis myotis* and *M. emarginatus* have declined to such low numbers, recovery may be impossible. However, although *M. dasycneme* has lost many nurseries, sufficient remain to ensure viable populations. It is most important to identify all nurseries and hibernacula and to give them adequate protection. This should include identification of surrounding key feeding areas and their subsequent management. *M. dasycneme* is endangered worldwide and the Netherlands is one of only three countries which shelter significant populations (the others being Denmark and USSR).

Legislation and Conservation Measures

Some measure of protection was afforded to bats in 1880, but the Nature Conservancy Act gave full protection in October 1973. This Act, which falls to the Ministry of Agriculture and Fisheries for implementation, not only protects bats but also their roosts. It is illegal to damage roosts or disturb bats which live there. Licences are issued for research, filming and photography. The keeping of species by the public is not permitted.

Thus, in principle, all bat roosts including nurseries, are protected, but feeding habitat is not.

The timber treatment industry is beginning to respond to the needs of nature conservation and public pressure. From 1989 pentachlorphenol and Lindane will be prohibited, but already some private companies have changed to using relatively non-toxic pyrethroid insecticides and borester fungicides.

Education

No country has surpassed the Netherlands in efforts to implement their bat protection legislation. In seven years over 300,000 leaflets, 30,000 posters, 21,000 stickers and 5,000 bat box booklets were circulated. In addition, two books were produced about bats and their conservation, one aimed specifically at children.

An enthusiastic bat group of about 100 amateurs is helping with education and bat conservation.

Special awards are presented to those persons or Institutions, who carry out particularly important bat conservation projects.

Research

Long term monitoring of hibernation sites is being continued with the aid of the bat group. New research is being initiated to record the distribution of bats in summer, with specific attention given to migration and natural history of *Pipistrellus nathusii.*

Bibliography

* Daan, S., Glas, G.H. and Voute, A.M. eds (1980) De Nederlandse vleermuizen. Bestandsontwikkelingen in winter - en zomerkwartieren. *Lutra.* 22, 1-118.

* Glas, G.H. (1986) Atlas van de Nederlandse vleermuizen 1970-1984, alsmede een vergelijking met vroegere gegevens *Zool. Bijdr.* 34, 1-97.

* Heijnen, A. and Voute, A.M. (1987) *Vleermuizen Natuurwerkboek.* (I.V.N.) De Volharding B.V., Amsterdam.

* Lina, P.H.C. (1981) The application of legal and practical protection of bats in the Netherlands. *Myotis.* 18-19. 19-22.

16
Belgium

Since the 1960s there has been a steady development of studies of the distribution and abundance of bats in Belgium. Some of these in the north east near Kanne, were a continuation of observations made by biologists over 25 years previously. Many large bat colonies were known in caves in the Ardennes, notably *Myotis myotis*, *Rhinolophus ferrumequinum* and *R. hipposideros*, but these have disappeared or declined to low numbers.

Co-ordination of research and conservation is maintained by Dr J. Fairon, Institute Royal des Sciences Naturelles de Belgique, Rue Vautier 29, B-1040 Bruxelles. Although bats are protected in most of Belgium, a separate administrative area which includes Brussels has not enacted legislation.

Threats

Possible destruction of the Caster limestone mines, threatens about 2,000 bats of up to 13 species. Limestone quarrying by a cement factory has already destroyed some of these tunnels, especially in the Netherlands, but the 50 kilometres of remaining galleries are vital for bats which migrate from three, possibly five countries.

Pollution and destruction of other caves and mines has caused loss of bats, as has disturbance by speleologists and tourists in those sites. House improvements which often involve building new rooms in roof spaces, is thought to have contributed to population declines.

Belgian Bats and their Status

Scientific and Local Name	Frequency of Occurrence	Status
Rhinolophus ferrumequinum (Grand rhinolophe)	Very rare, occurs in south east	E
Rhinolophus hipposideros (Petit rhinolophe)	Very rare, small numbers in south east	E
Myotis mystacinus (Vespertilion à moustache)	Fairly rare everywhere	I
Myotis brandtii (Vespertilion de Brandt)	Rare, probably throughout country	I
Myotis emarginatus (Vespertilion émarginé)	Rare, declining, occurs mostly in south	E
Myotis daubentonii (Vespertilion de Daubenton)	Probably common everywhere	?Nt
Myotis dasycneme (Vespertilion des marais)	Few scattered records	E
Myotis nattereri (Vespertilion de Natterer)	Rare, mainly in east	I
Myotis bechsteinii (Vespertilion de Bechstein)	Very few records	I
Myotis myotis (Grand murin)	Rare and declining	E
Pipistrellus pipistrellus (Pipistrelle commune)	Very common throughout	Nt
Pipistrellus nathusii (Pipistrellus de Nathusius)	Rare, recent increase in number of records	I
Eptesicus serotinus (Sérotine commune)	Fairly rare everywhere	E
Nyctalus noctula (Noctule commune)	Fairly rare, declining	I(?E)
Nyctalus leisleri (Noctule de Leisler)	Few records, status unknown	I
Plecotus auritus (Oreillard commun)	Fairly common, widespread, declining	E
Plecotus austriacus (Oreillard gris)	Very rare everywhere	E
Barbastella barbastellus (Barbastelle)	Rarely recorded	E

stone mine near Mons, 'La Malogne', has State protection by the Water and Forest Service, but the large entrances are open and many people visit the 15 kilometres of tunnel, causing disturbance. Bat populations have declined to about 150 individuals, from many hundreds 30 years ago.

Legislation

Belgium has three main administrative regions for nature conservation. Bats were given legislative protection for Flanders in September 1980 and Wallonie in March 1983. However, bats are not yet protected in the Brussels region and this is an urgent need. Legislation protects bats from capture and killing, also their roosts. It is illegal to transport the animals or sell them, whether dead or alive.

Education

There has been little public education about the needs of bat conservation. Development of amateur bat groups should be able to help, by producing information in both official languages.

Research

Continued monitoring of the important hibernacula around the Caster quarries combined with results from other sites, will coincide with similar work in other parts of Europe. There is a need for more detailed survey work on the endangered bat species, especially the *Rhinolophus* spp., *M. myotis* and *M. emarginatus*, to find and secure their roosts and feeding habitat.

Bibliography

- Fairon, J., Gilson, R., Jooris, R., Faber, T. and Meisch, C. (1982) Cartographie provisoire de la faune chiropterologique belgo - Luxembourgeoise. Bull. Cent. Baguement. Recherche. Cheiropt. Belgique 7, 1-125.

17
Luxembourg

No report has been received. However, the species composition and conservation problems are similar to those in Belgium and surrounding countries.

All bats and their roosts were protected by the Grand-Ducal regulations of November 1972.

18
Great Britain

Two studies involving bat ringing began in the late 1940s one of which continues, but there has been relatively little research on bats. Historically, bats in Britain were generally neglected by naturalists and only in the 1980s has there been a substantial development of interest. This former lack of interest means there is very little documentation of previous population distribution or abundance. However, efforts are being made to assess population changes both past and present. This information is being collated by Dr R E Stebbings and Mr H R Arnold, Institute of Terrestrial Ecology, Monks Wood Experimental Station, Abbots Ripton, Huntingdon, PE17 2LS.

As a result of experiences in the Netherlands, biologists in Britain became aware in the late 1950s of declines caused by bat ringing and observer disturbance. Consequently the Mammal Society co-ordinated the design and field trials of different styles of rings manufactured from a variety of materials. As a result, by 1970 one type was found which caused no damage to the most sensitive species, *Rhinolophus ferrumequinum*. Ring designs were refined still further to the point where, if correctly applied, they cause no damage to bats. These rings are manufactured by Lambournes (Birmingham) Ltd., Colman House, Station Road, Knowle, Solihull, West Midlands, B93 OHL, and are supplied to countries throughout the world.

In the early 1960s, when it was realised some bat populations were declining, several hundred educational leaflets were distributed annually, largely in response to requests for help with bat problems. In 1969, the number of enquiries totalled over 900. Following extensive media publicity about bat conservation, in

British Bats and their Status

Scientific and Local Name	Frequency of Occurrence	Status
Rhinolophus ferrumequinum (Greater horseshoe bat)	Very rare, occurs in south west	E
Rhinolophus hipposideros (Lesser horseshoe bat)	Rare, found in Wales and south west England	E
Myotis mystacinus (Whiskered bat)	Common in west and north England, rare/absent elsewhere	V
Myotis brandtii (Brandt's bat)	Common in west and north England, rare/absent elsewhere	V
Myotis daubentonii (Daubenton's bat)	Common throughout Britain	Nt
Myotis nattereri (Natterer's bat)	Fairly common throughout Britain	V
Myotis bechsteinii (Bechstein's bat)	Rare in central southern England, absent elsewhere	R
Myotis myotis (Mouse-eared bat)	Only one specimen remaining (Jan 1987)	E(ex)
Pipistrellus pipistrellus (Pipistrelle)	Very common everywhere	Nt
Pipistrellus nathusii (Nathusius' pipistrelle)	Vagrant, three records	--
Eptesicus serotinus (Serotine)	Widespread in southern Britain, declining in south east England	V
Eptesicus nilssonii (Northern bat)	A single vagrant in 1987	--
Vespertilio murinus (Parti-coloured bat)	Very rare vagrant	--
Nyctalus noctula (Noctule)	Rare in some lowlands but common in well wooded areas	V
Nyctalus leisleri (Leisler's bat)	Rare, widespread in England and Wales	I
Plecotus auritus (Brown long-eared bat)	Very common, occurs throughout Britain	Nt
Plecotus austriacus (Grey long-eared bat)	Very rare, a few small colonies in south of England	V(?E)
Barbastella barbastellus (Barbastelle)	Very rare but widespread. No colonies known	I

1970 (European Conservation Year) the number of enquiries fell to about 250 per year and often many of these people showed an interest in helping bats rather than wanting to get rid of them. In 1971 more than 3,000 bat boxes and information packs were sold to the public in conjunction with the World Wildlife Fund (UK). Since 1981, when all bats were given legal protection, a large number of people have become interested in their conservation.

*Plate 12. Bechstein's bat, **Myotis bechsteinii**, one of Europe's rarest bats. Found widely, but very few specimens. Being a species of large forests, it is difficult to find, and, as with several species, it may not be as rare as is thought at present (photo: R. E. Stebbings).*

Surveys of house bats conducted throughout Britain from 1978 to 1987, show the most common species *Pipistrellus pipistrellus* has declined by about 60 per cent. This decline has not occurred evenly countrywide as results from Scotland suggest colony size there has increased.

Threats

Three major types of problem face bats in Britain. Firstly landscape changes, involving loss of pasture, deciduous woodland and especially hollow trees in woods and hedgerows, are likely to have had a serious impact on roost and insect abundance.

Secondly, the use of pesticides in buildings has killed many bats. These chemicals continue to present a serious problem, even though low toxicity products are becoming more popular. Cavity wall insulation, repointing walls, and renovating bridges and old buildings, are likely to be killing many bats and excluding others. Although annually many thousands of bats were deliberately killed in the past, it is thought this number has been reduced considerably by the recent improved knowledge about bat conservation.

Thirdly, large numbers of mines are being solidly capped. These sites are very important both for hibernation in the winter and nurseries in some warmer entrances in the summer.

Key Sites

Hibernation

Only 17 sites are known to shelter more than 100 bats in hibernation, all distributed in southern Britain. North Wales has two, south Wales two, Midlands one, East Anglia three, south east England two and south west England seven. These sites include three caves, nine mines, two brick lined tunnels and three cellars or ice-houses associated with buildings. There are approximately 250,000 metalliferous mine shafts and a similar number of coal mines in Britain. Only a few have been surveyed but a large number shelter bats both in summer and winter. Many of the caves, mines and cellars used by the endangered *Rhinolophus* spp., are key sites requiring protection, to ensure the survival of those species.

Summer

Twelve nursery sites are known for the endangered *R. ferrumequinum* which have over five young born each year. In Britain, the total number of recorded births was about 700 in 1987 from a population of about 3,000 bats. Similarly, for *R. hipposideros* which may nationally total about 8,000 bats, all breeding sites are important because Britain is one of the remaining strongholds for the species.

No special feeding habitats have been identified but some of these should be defined, especially around nurseries of the endangered species.

Protected Sites

Relatively very few roosts have been specially protected for bats. However about 50, mostly cave and mine sites, have been grilled to prevent unauthorised access. Degradation and loss of key sites is a cause for concern especially for the endangered species. The governmental agency responsible for the implementation of the wildlife legislation, the Nature Conservancy Council (NCC), has devised criteria to assess whether a site should receive protection as a Site of Special Scientific Interest (SSSI).

For *R. ferrumequinum*, all (main) nurseries are to be safeguarded, together with winter sites with 50 or more bats counted on one occasion or 20 per cent of a colony. In fact these figures are too high because important sites are being lost to these bats due to over disturbance by casual visitors. Preventing the disturbance will allow numbers to increase again. To ensure survival of these rare species, all sites which contain 15 bats or five per cent of a colony, should receive both legal and physical protection.

Under present SSSI criteria, *R. hipposideros* nursery sites containing 100 or more bats and hibernacula with at least 50 bats, will receive SSSI protection. However, being a critically endangered species in much of northern Europe, the minimum criteria for deciding on statutory protection of its roosts should be considerably lower, perhaps 30 bats for nurseries and 20 bats in hibernacula.

There are also suggested criteria for assessing the importance of sites containing more common species. If a hibernation site contains at least 50 bats of four species, or over 100 bats of three species, or 150 bats of two species, then it qualifies for legal protection. Again these figures may be too high, as nationally there are very few sites which qualify and a sliding scale depending on latitude may be required. Generally all the large populations are in the south, with only a few hibernacula containing small numbers of bats known in northern England or Scotland.

Conservation of Endangered Species

Sufficient detailed research has been carried out on the two *Rhinolophus* spp., to enable an effective conservation strategy to be produced. There is a need for more research, to identify critical feeding habitat surrounding key roosts. This is required because changes in land use may adversely affect insect populations, thereby causing further declines in numbers of bats an area can support. Both species are isolated from other European populations, so effective conservation does not depend on other States.

Legislation

Two species of bat were protected in 1975, (*R. ferrumequinum* and *M. myotis*), but all species were more comprehensively covered under the Wildlife and Countryside Act 1981. This enactment protected bats and their roosts and prevented disturbance to both. As it is also an offence to damage a roost even when bats are not present, embodied within the Act was a requirement for people wishing to get rid of bats, or those about to undertake building or other operations which might affect bats, to contact the NCC for advice. To some extent this legislation has worked well in highlighting the need for care in renovating property, but most timber treatment specialists have never sought advice although they must come across bat colonies. Either deliberately or through ignorance they fail to do what the law requires, which is to notify the NCC when signs of bats are discovered. There have been several successful prosecutions under the Act, with fines up to £1,000, but the wording of the legislation effectively makes it impossible to implement. In most cases an 'Intentional' act has to be proved (or admitted). In British law the word 'reckless' is much more appropriate, therefore a change in the wording is required before bats will be adequately protected.

Education

Since the Wildlife Act was passed in 1981, a national network of approximately 60 bat groups has developed with a membership of about 1,500 people. These groups are co-ordinated by a secretariat based at the Flora and Fauna Preservation Society (FFPS), (c/o Zoological Society of London, Regents Park, London NW1 4RY) serving a national panel comprising representatives from the bat groups, FFPS, NCC, Mammal Society, governmental bat research biologists and non-governmental conservation organisations.

The groups are a vital part of the bat conservation movement because members are often asked by the NCC to visit sites where advice is required. Information is subsequently reported back to the NCC which provides the appropriate advice. Also, the local groups provide an important source of manpower for surveys, as well as education for schools and various interest groups.

Both the statutory agency and voluntary bodies produce and disseminate educative materials. The increasing amount of publications reflects the developing interest in bats. From 1962 to 1970 about 5,000 leaflets were distributed, but in the following ten years about 100,000 were distributed with a similar number up to the end of 1986. During this time the range of material widened from a simple leaflet, to a variety of general and specialist topics including species leaflets, bat box booklets, films, videos, audiovisual slide packs and identification keys.

Research

The most important need is for surveys, to identify sites and to monitor them. Further studies should investigate the food and feeding requirements for each species, to enable adequate provision to be made for habitat protection in conservation plans.

Bibliography

- Mitchell-Jones, A.J., Jefferies, D.J., Stebbings, R.E. and Arnold, H.R. (1986) Public concern about bats (Chiroptera) in Britain: an analysis of enquiries 1982-1983. *Biol Conserv.* 36, 315-328.

- Stebbings, R.E. and Griffith, F. (1986) *Distribution and status of bats in Europe.* Institute of Terrestrial Ecology, Huntingdon.

- Stebbings, R.E. and Jefferies, D.J. (1982) *Focus on Bats.* Nature Conservancy Council, Peterborough.

19

Northern Ireland

There have been few studies of bats in Northern Ireland and little is known about the distribution and abundance of species. Since the wildlife legislation (Wildlife (NI) Order 1985) came into force in 1986, attention has focused on this lack of knowledge and some research has begun. The Countryside and Wildlife branch of the Department of the Environment, Stormont, Belfast, has devolved some of its administrative responsibility in implementing the legislation (which closely resembles Great Britain's Wildlife and Countryside Act). Some of the advisory role, including documentation and development of a site register is being performed under contract c/o Mr Marshall McKee, Ulster Museum, Botanic Gardens, Belfast, BJ9 5AB.

An amateur bat group affiliated to those in Great Britain, is rapidly improving knowledge about the State's bats. There is a need for increased survey and monitoring work and the development of a conservation programme. Of particular concern, is the long term conservation of *Nyctalus leisleri*, which is more abundant in Ireland than anywhere else in its range.

Bats of Northern Ireland and their Status

Scientific and Local Name	Frequency of Occurrence	Status
Myotis mystacinus (Whiskered bat)	Very rare everywhere	R
Myotis daubentonii (Daubenton's bat)	Probably abundant everywhere	Nt
Myotis nattereri (Natterer's bat)	Rare, probably widespread	V
Pipistrellus pipistrellus (Pipistrelle)	Very common	Nt
Nyctalus leisleri (Leisler's bat)	Common throughout	V
Plecotus auritus (Brown long-eared bat)	Very common everywhere	N

Note: One record suggests *Myotis brandtii* may occur.

20
Eire

Until 1984 little was known about the distribution or status of bats in Eire. There had been no detailed research studies, but Irish naturalists earlier this century made significant discoveries about aspects of the natural history of their bats. In 1984, the Forest and Wildlife Service initiated a national bat survey. This is continuing and is co-ordinated by Mr P.J. O'Sullivan, Drumcliffe, Ennis, Co Clare.

Ireland has a considerable population of *Nyctalus leisleri* which occurs everywhere. One colony in Cork totals approximately 1,000 bats. This species is not common in any other area of its range. Also, *Rhinolophus hipposideros* is a locally common bat in western parts of the country. With an estimated population of up to 10,000 bats, it too, is of special significance in the European context. Both these species need careful consideration because of the overall importance of the populations.

One of the colonies of *R. hipposideros* is possibly one of the largest remaining in western Europe and has increased recently to over 400 bats.

Threats

Each year there are hundreds of severe cases of river pollution, mostly caused by agricultural effluent particularly from silage. These incidents destroy the water based insects which are an important food source for bats and continues to be a serious threat to colonies. Organochlorine pesticides, used in remedial timber treatments are known to kill bats.

Bats of Eire and their Status

Scientific and Local Name	Frequency of Occurrence	Status
Rhinolophus hipposideros (Lesser horseshoe bat) (Mion-ialtóg chrúshtónach)	Common in west and south west, absent elsewhere	V
Myotis mystacinus (Whiskered bat) (Ialtóg ghiobach)	Uncommon, mostly found in south	V
Myotis daubentonii (Daubenton's bat) (Ialtóg Dhaubenton)	Probably common everywhere	Nt
Myotis nattereri (Natterer's bat) (Ialtóg Natterer)	Probably common everywhere	V
Pipistrellus pipistrellus (Pipistrelle) (Ialtóg phipistríneach)	Very common throughout	Bt
Nyctalus leisleri (Leisler's bat) (Ialtóg Leisler)	Common everywhere	V
Plecotus auritus (Brown long-eared bat) (Ialtóg Fhadchluasach)	Common everywhere	V

Key Sites

All the breeding sites for *R. hipposideros* can be regarded as vital for the long term survival of this locally distributed species. Also many of the known hibernation sites need protection. Some cave sites were protected several years ago following rapid declines in the numbers of bats using them. Subsequently, numbers recovered and steady increases are being recorded each year.

The feeding habitat for the largest colonies of *R. hipposideros* needs to be identified and protected. Most large colonies occur in sheltered scrub and well wooded areas and these should be safeguarded.

Because of the worldwide importance of the species in Eire, a representative sample of *N. leisleri* colonies should receive protection.

Protection of Sites

A number of caves sheltering hibernating *R. hipposideros* are already protected with grilles and more are planned. Two buildings are partially protected because they contain the largest colonies of the two species detailed above.

Legislation and Conservation Measures

The Wildlife Act, passed in 1976, provided protection to bats and their roosts. Licences are required for research activities including ringing.

Implementation of the legislation, especially in relation to protection of sites, is hampered by lack of sufficient funding, although very efficient use is made of the present meagre resources. Conservation measures already taken have been most successful and an increased budget would help ensure a long term future for the two most significant species.

Education

Following initiation of the National bat survey, a lot of publicity was given by the media. As a result, public attitudes to bats were changed very quickly. Of over 400 enquiries in the first year, 90 per cent wished to get rid of bats, but this pattern was completely reversed two years later when 90 per cent of people seeking advice were happy to keep the bats, and often wanted information on how to attract bats to their houses or gardens.

Amateur bat groups are being formed, but progress is slow.

21
Isle of Man

There have been no systematic studies of bats in the Isle of Man, but some occasional observations have been made. The Island is one of the few places remaining in Europe where bats are not protected by legislation, but proposals are in preparation. Information about bats and their conservation is gathered by Dr L.S. Garrad, The Manx Museum, Douglas.

In the mid 1940s, a diligent naturalist well known for the accuracy of his observations, visited a church in a sheltered wooded valley to the west of Douglas. He caught one cluster of roosting bats in a hand net and estimated there were another 20 to 30. The net contained 700 bats, mostly *Myotis nattereri* with a few *M. mystacinus*(sl) and *Plecotus auritus*. From these observations the population was estimated to number at least 14,000 bats. Corroboration of the cluster size was given independently, when the church authorities admitted the bats had been gassed in the last 25 years by a pest control company from mainland Britain. From the volume of dead bodies an estimate suggests between 12,000 and 15,000 bats were killed. Some 200 to 300 bats were estimated to remain in other parts of the building in 1987. No other *M. nattereri* colonies have been found on the Island, so the building may have sheltered most of the animals of that species.

Passing and implementing legislation is essential if this type of problem is to be avoided.

Bats of the Isle of Man and their Status

Scientific and Local Name	Frequency of Occurrence	Status
Myotis mystacinus sl (Whiskered bat)	Rare, no recent records	?
Myotis nattereri (Natterer's bat)	Rare	V
Pipistrellus pipistrellus (Pipistrelle)	Common occurs everywhere	Nt
Plecotus auritus (Brown long-eared bat)	Fairly common Occurs everywhere	V

Bibliography

• Wagstaffe, R. (1979) Looking for bats. *Proc. Liverpool Nats. Field Club*. (1970-1978).

22
States of Guernsey

Some recent observations suggest there are several colonies of bats on the Island, as well as on Alderney and Herm. It is likely a number of bats interchange between the various Channel Islands and with mainland France. Although there are persistent reports of *Rhinolophus ferrumequinum*, the Island is probably too small to sustain a colony.

There is no formal bat group on Guernsey but co-ordination is being achieved by Mrs P. Costen, La Broderie, Route de la Claire Mare, St. Pierre du Bois.

At present bats are not protected and the State is not a party to the Bern or Bonn Conventions. There is a clear need to enact legislation protecting bats and their roosts, and to protect the few roosts housing colonies.

Naturalists who are already interested in bats are attempting, with some success, to ensure harmful timber treatment chemicals are replaced with the less toxic pyrethroids.

Bats of Guernsey and their Status

Scientific and Local Name	Frequency of Occurrence	Status
Rhinolophus ferrumequinum (Greater horseshoe bat)	Probably a vagrant	?
Pipistrellus pipistrellus (Pipistrelle)	Common everywhere	V
Plecotus austriacus (Grey long-eared bat)	Fairly common widespread	V

23

States of Jersey

A developing interest in bats by a few people in the 1980s has enabled them to find a number of bat roosts occupied in the summer, but hibernation sites are unknown. Proximity of the Island to mainland France suggests that some bats may be migrants. The first *Pipistrellus nathusii* was recorded in December 1987. A single newly born juvenile *Eptesicus serotinus* was found, but no other bats of this species have been seen.

A bat group is developing activities including education and site recording. This is co-ordinated by Mr J. B. Carroll, Jersey Wildlife Preservation Trust, Les Augres Manor, Trinity.

Jersey is not party to either the Bonn or Bern Conventions and bats do not have legal protection on the Island. However, a wildlife conservation law is in preparation.

The main threats to bats are toxic chemicals used in building renovation for remedial timber treatments, and pesticides sprayed on crops.

Only one breeding colony is known for *Plecotus austriacus*. This site, a building, needs protection.

Bats of Jersey and their Status

Scientific and Local Name	Frequency of Occurrence	Status
Rhinolophus ferrumequinum (Greater horseshoe bat)	Vagrant	?
Pipistrellus pipistrellus (Pipistrelle)	Common everywhere	V
Pipistrellus nathusii (Nathusius' pipistrelle)	Vagrant, one record	--
Eptesicus serotinus (Serotine)	Vagrant, one record	--
Plecotus austriacus (Grey long-eared)	Rare, occurs everywhere	V

24
Portugal

Bats have received little attention, consequently information on their distribution and status is poor. Nevertheless recent observations show there are a number of extensive cave populations and these are being disturbed by people. As the Iberian peninsula appears to have some of the largest concentrations of cave dwelling bats in Europe, there is an urgent need to undertake surveys, identify the important roosts and effect adequate conservation measures.

*Plate 13. Brown long-eared bat, **Plecotus auritus**, one of two species of long-eared bats in Europe. More common in the north, it is a woodland species now commonly found living in roof spaces of houses. It is often the first species to find bat roost boxes.*

Portuguese Bats and their Status

Scientific and Local Name	Frequency of Occurrence	Status
Rhinolophus ferrumequinum (Morcego de ferradura grande)	Fairly rare in north, possibly absent in south	E
Rhinolophus hipposideros (Morcego de ferradura pequeno)	Fairly rare throughout	E
Rhinolophus euryale (Morcego de ferradura mediterrânico)	Fairly common in north	E
Rhinolophus mehelyi (Morcego de ferradura mourisco)	Rare, mostly in south	E
Myotis mystacinus (Morcego de bigodes)	Only one record	K
Myotis emarginatus (Morcego lanudo)	Very rare everywhere	E
Myotis daubentonii (Morcego d'água)	Common everywhere	Nt
Myotis nattereri (Morcego de franja)	Very rare	E
Myotis bechsteinii (Morcego de Bechstein)	Very rare	R
Myotis myotis (Morcego rato grande)	Common in north, rare in south	E
Myotis blythi (Morcego rato pequeno)	Common in south, rare in north	E
Pipistrellus pipistrellus (Morcego anáo)	Very common throughout	Nt
Pipistrellus nathusii (Morcego de Nathusius)	Doubtful occurrence	K
Pipistrellus kuhli (Morcego dc Kuhl)	Common everywhere	Nt
Pipistrellus savii (Morcego de Savi)	Only one record	K

Portuguese Bats and their Status

Scientific and Local Name	Frequency of Occurrence	Status
Eptesicus serotinus (Morcego ortelao)	Common throughout	Nt
Nyctalus noctula (Morcego arboricola grande)	Very rare	V
Nyctalus leisleri (Morcego aboricola pequeno)	Uncommon everywhere	V
Nyctalus lasiopterus (Morcego arboricola gigante)	Only one record, vagrant?	K
Miniopterus schreibersii (Morcego de peluche)	Very common everywhere	V
Plecotus auritus (Morcego orechudo castanho)	Very rare	R
Plecotus austriacus (Morcego orechudo cinzento)	Very common	V
Barbastella barbastellus (Morcego negro)	Only one record	K
Tadarida teniotis (Morcego rabudo)	Fairly rare throughout	V

The Portugese Parks Service recently initiated a programme of surveys, assessment and protection, in co-operation with Dr J.M. Palmerim, Departamento de Zoologia, Universidade de Lisboa, 1700 Lisboa.

Although few detailed observations have been made, large cave colonies are known for three species. Clusters containing more than 1,000 bats have been reported for *Myotis myotis*, *M. blythi* and *Miniopterus schreibersii*. One colony of the latter has been estimated at 20,000 animals.

Threats

By far the most important is disturbance of bats in caves by speleologists and casual visitors. This is especially relevant in the busy tourist area of the Algarve, where holiday-makers frequently visit such caves.

Felling of the cork oak (*Quercus suber*) woodlands may be affecting some species of bat dependent on broad-leaved forests, but no-one has studied this possibility.

Key Sites

All the large cave colonies are in need of identification and protection. Many of these colonies may be of international importance, as it is likely some bats migrate in autumn, to Spain and north Africa. Some of the most important sites are listed here:

◘ Minas de Sto. Adriao. Breeding colonies with several thousand *M. myotis*, *M. blythi* and *M. schreibersii*. This is the only cave holding large colonies of bats in the north.

◘ Gruta dos Morcegos. Large colonies of *M. schreibersii*, *M. myotis*, *M. mehelyi* and *Rhinolophus euryale*.

◘ Olhos d'Agua do Alviela. This cave contains at least nine species, with large breeding colonies of *M. schreibersii*, *M. myotis*, *M. emarginatus* and *R. euryale*.

◘ Casa da Moura. Large numbers of *M. schreibersii* and *R. euryale*.

◘ Algar do Ladoeiro. Contains at least five species with a breeding and wintering colony of thousands of *M. schreibersii*.

◘ Algar des Gralhas. Large breeding colonies of *M. schreibersii* and probably *R. mehelyi*, with five other species.

◘ Cova da Moura. The breeding colony of *M. schreibersii* here reaches about 20,000 individuals.

◘ Fojo dos Morcegos. Shelters large numbers of *M. schreibersii* and *M. myotis*.

▢ Gruta da Amarela. Breeding colony of more than 100 *R. ferrumequinum.*

▢ Mina das Furnazinhas. Breeding colonies with hundreds of *M. blythi* and *R. mehelyi.*

▢ Grutas de Ibnamar. Summer and winter roosts for over 100 *R. mehelyi*, sometimes with *R. hipposideros.*

▢ Igrejinha de Sóidos. Contains large numbers of *M. schreibersii* and *M. blythi.*

▢ Lapa da Rocha da Pena. A breeding colony of several thousand *M. schreibersii*, with large numbers of *M. blythi* and *R. mehelyi.*

▢ Salustreira Grande. Thousands of bats present at different times of the year. Mostly *M. schreibersii* but also *M. blythi, R. mehelyi* and *R. hipposideros.*

All these are vitally important. They need protection and careful management to allow legitimate use by cavers and others, without compromising the nature conservation interest.

Legislation

Many of Portugal's bats were protected in 1967, but the Decree did not list all species now known to live there. In 1974, further legislation was enacted which specified species of wildlife which could be hunted. By inference, other wildlife species were protected. This lack of special protection for bats may make it difficult to implement effective protection. Also, the legislation does not give protection to roost sites. Because Portugal has ratified the Bern and Bonn Conventions, the State recognises the clear obligation to provide adequate legislation to protect bats, their roosts and habitats.

Education

Efforts are being made to inform cave visitors and especially speleologists, about bats. However, a more extensive education programme is required, especially in holiday resorts, to try to limit disturbance to cave colonies. A survey is under-way mainly amongst cavers, to find the sites used by bats and to discover whether there is historic knowledge of population size in any site.

Research

Regular monitoring of the important sites is needed, as well as research to identify the associated feeding habitats.

Bibliography

Palmeirim, J.M. (1987)   Status of bats in Portugal. *m.s. University of Lisboa.*

25
Gibraltar

A survey of tunnels, caves and buildings from 1958 to 1984 revealed 56 sites were occupied by bats. Nine of the roosts held more than 1,000 bats with a total of over 6,000 bats being recorded in two sites, 'Devil's Fall' and 'Martins' caves. There were at least 38 clusters, each containing over 100 bats.

Many of the roosts have been disturbed both by local people and tourists. A repeat survey in 1986, showed at least twelve sites had been destroyed. Also, reports have been received of a colony, once estimated to consist of 5,000 *Miniopterus schreibersii* in Martins Cave, having been smoked out and killed by local young people. Only 20 bats remained in 1986.

Bats are not protected in Gibraltar, therefore it is vital to effect legislation as well as to implement protection of all remaining colonies. The earlier survey suggested the total bat population was about 33,000 bats, but almost certainly many of those seasonally migrated to other countries. None of the large colonies has been seen in the last five years.

It is important to initiate a survey to establish which sites remain important to bats and to monitor them.

It may be necessary to protect sites which formerly contained large roosts, but where disturbance has caused bats to leave. Experience elsewhere has shown that by creating such sanctuaries, bats are quickly encouraged to return.

As well as the need for legislation, an education programme should be directed at all inhabitants, especially those who own or visit roosts, often with parties of tourists. Usually it is possible to maintain traditional activities while avoiding the critical areas used by bats.

Bats of Gibraltar and their Status

Scientific and Local Name	Frequency of Occurrence	Status
Rhinolophus hipposideros (Lesser horseshoe bat)	One record, possibly a vagrant	?
Myotis myotis (Mouse-eared bat)	Common	E
Pipistrellus pipistrellus (Pipistrelle)	Common	E
Miniopterus schreibersii (Schreiber's bat)	Common	E
Tadrida teniotis (European free-tailed bat)	One record only	?

26
Spain

Over 200 reports have been published giving information about the distribution of bats in Spain. But despite this there is no clear picture either of the distribution or abundance of most species. Almost all papers give details of where bats were found and describe the types of roosts, but rarely is there any indication of numbers of bats. For this reason there is virtually no information on the status of species. However, local extinctions have been reported. *Rhinolophus ferrumequinum* is now extinct on the Balearic Island of Eivissa (Ibiza), and also probably on the adjacent Formentera. *Myotis myotis* appears to be extinct on Eivissa.

Since 1980 there has been a substantial increase in the number of people studying bats, many with an interest in conservation. One of the biologists concerned with site protection is Dr J. Benzal, Catedra de Zoologia des Vertebrados, Universidad Complutense, 28040, Madrid.

An extensive study involving the ringing of over 11,000 bats was conducted from 1976 to 1986. This showed individuals of *M. myotis*, *M. blythi* and *Miniopterus schreibersii*, moved from 200 to 600 kilometres between roosts. Unfortunately, poor quality rings were used and many bats received injuries.

Threats

Most threats are similar to those in other countries. Bats are excluded or killed in buildings and caves and loss of forest by felling and fires is likely to be affecting species which depend on those types of habitat. Disturbance and killing of bats in the

Spanish Bats and their Status

Scientific and Local Name	Frequency of Occurrence	Status
Rhinolophus ferrumequinum (Murciélago grande de herradura)	Fairly common everywhere	V
Rhinolophus hipposideros (Murciélago pequeño herradura)	Fairly common everywhere	V
Rhinolophus euryale (Murciélago mediterráneo de herradura)	Fairly common everywhere	V
Rhinolophus mehelyi (Murciélago mediano de herradura)	Absent in north west, most common in south and east	K
Myotis mystacinus (Murciélago bigotudo)	Rare in central northern areas, absent elsewhere	I
Myotis emarginatus (Murciélago de Geoffroy)	Rare everywhere	I
Myotis capaccinii (Murciélago patudo)	Rare, east coast only	K
Myotis daubentonii (Murciélago ribereño)	Abundant everywhere	Nt
Myotis nattereri (Murciélago de Natterer)	Rare but widespread	K
Myotis bechsteinii (Murciélago de Bechstein)	Few scattered records	R
Myotis myotis (Murciélago ratonero grande)	Common throughout country	V
Myotis blythi (Murciélago ratonero mediano)	Found everywhere, common in south	V
Pipistrellus pipistrellus (Murciélago común)	Common everywhere	Nt
Pipistrellus nathusii (Murciélago de Nathusius)	No recent records, ? winter immigrant	I(?Ex)

Spanish Bats and their Status (continued)

Scientific and Local Name	Frequency of Occurrence	Status
Pipistrellus kuhli (Murciélago de borde claro)	Absent in north, fairly rare elsewhere	K
Pipistrellus savii (Murciélago montañero)	Scattered records, perhaps absent in south west	K
Eptesicus serotinus (Murciélago hortelano)	Fairly common everywhere	I
Nyctalus noctula (Nóctulo común)	A few scattered records in north	R
Nyctalus leisleri (Nóctula pequeño)	Rare, found in highlands	K
Nyctalus lasiopterus (Nóctulo gigante)	Rare, a few scattered records	K
Miniopterus schreibersii (Murciélago de cueva)	Common everywhere	V
Plecotus auritus (Orejudo septentrional)	Rare, found mostly in northern highlands	V
Plecotus austriacus (Orejudo meridional)	Fairly common everywhere	K
Barbastella barbastellus (Murciélago de bosque)	Very rare, occurs in north	I
Tadarida teniotis (Murciélago rabudo)	Rare, occurs throughout	K

large vulnerable cave colonies is causing concern and shows the need to protect important sites.

Key Sites

Information is only now being gathered on the sites which are most important for the conservation of bats in Spain. Clearly many caves which contain large colonies will require protection, especially those linked on migration routes. *M. myotis, M. blythi* and *M. schreibersii* are all known to be migratory, consequently further study will be required to identify those key sites.

Legislation

Bats were protected by Decree from 1981. However, only bats are protected and not their roosts and feeding habitat. Spain has ratified the Bern and Bonn Conventions and is therefore committed to enact appropriate legislation. After this first step, implementation will be required. At present the National Institute for the Conservation of Nature (ICONA) has jurisdiction over the conservation of species in National Parks, but this responsibility needs to be extended to cover all the land surface of Spain.

Education and Research

There have been a few excellent popular articles about bats in conservation magazines, but no widely circulated leaflets or other material. It is very important that this should be done, as well as the setting up of a bat conservation forum to discuss and disseminate information.

There is also an urgent need to undertake surveys and initiate monitoring programmes, to link with observations being made in adjacent States.

Bibliography

- Molina, J.A.M.de., and Sanz, P.S. (1986) Los Murciélagos: un mundo aparte. *Vida Silvestre* (ICONA). 60, 220-233.

- Paz, O.de., Fernández, R., and Benzal, J. (1986) El anillamiento de quiropteros en el centro de la peninsula Iberica durante el periodo 1977-1986. *Bol. Estación Central de Ecología.* 30, 113-138.

27
France

There has been a long history of detailed studies into the biology, systematics and natural history of bats, extending over a century. From 1945 there was a wide ranging programme of bat ringing which resulted in over 120,000 animals being marked. In the 1950s, it was first noticed that some large cave colonies had declined dramatically, apparently due to tourism and vandalism. Since then, research has continued on a wide front and has led to the forming of an active movement of amateurs and professionals, concerned primarily with conservation problems. The co-ordinator for this group is Mr J. F. Noblet, Conseil National Chiroptères, c/o FRAPNA, 4, Rue Hector Belioz, 38000 Grenoble.

Since 1985, a campaign has developed to assess the conservation needs for bats and to undertake protective measures. Several organisations are helping with this task, including W.W.F., Federation of Nature Protection Societies and the Society for the Study and Protection of Mammals.

Threats

Remedial timber treatments are known to have killed many bats, including *Pipistrellus pipistrellus* and *Myotis myotis*. Whole colonies of *P. pipistrellus*, *Plecotus* spp., and *Eptesicus serotinus* are known to have been killed by domestic cats. Vandalism has often destroyed large numbers of bats. In 1986, 600 *Miniopterus schreibersii* were killed in the cave, 'Cabrespine' in the Department of Aude. (This cave shelters 60,000 bats in the winter). Severe winter weather is known to cause the deaths of many bats, while cold springs have resulted in colonies of *M. myotis* failing to reproduce.

Bats of France and their Status

Scientific and Local Name	Frequency of Occurrence	Status
Rhinolophus ferrumequinum (Grand Rhinolophe)	Fairly rare everywhere	E
Rhinolophus hipposideros (Petit Rhinolophe)	Fairly rare almost everywhere	E
Rhinolophus euryale (Rhinolophe euryale)	Rare, occurs east and west of Massif Central	E
Rhinolophus mehelyi (Rhinolophe de Mehely)	No recent records	Ex
Myotis mystacinus (Murin à moustaches)	Uncommon, absent in Jura and south	V
Myotis brandtii (Murin de Brandt)	Rare, occurs north east only	R
Myotis emarginatus (Murin oreilles échancrées)	Rare, widespread, not in north or south east	V
Myotis capaccinii (Murin Capaccini)	Rare, near Mediterranean	V
Myotis daubentonii (Murin de Daubenton)	Uncommon, widespread perhaps absent in south	V
Myotis dasycneme (Murin des marais)	Very rare, occurs only in north east	E
Myotis nattereri (murin de Natterer)	Uncommon but widespread	V
Myotis bechsteinii (Murin de Bechstein)	Very rare, few records	V
Myotis myotis (Grand murin)	Uncommon but widespread	E
Myotis blythi (Petit murin)	Rare, occurs mostly in south	E
Pipistrellus pipistrellus (Pipistrelle commune)	Common throughout	Nt

Bats of France and their Status (continued)

Scientific and Local Name	Frequency of Occurrence	Status
Pipistrellus nathusii (Pipistrelle de Nathusius)	Rare, mostly a winter visitor	V
Pipistrellus kuhli (Pipistrelle de Kuhl)	Uncommon, widespread except north east	Nt
Pipistrellus savii (Pipistrelle de Savi)	Common in south, especially in Corsica	V
Eptesicus serotinus (Sérotine commune)	Common almost everywhere	V
Eptesicus nilssonii (Sérotine de Nilsson)	Few records in extreme east	R
Vespertilio murinus (Sérotin bicolore)	Few records in east	R
Nyctalus noctula (Noctule commune)	Uncommon in north, absent in south	V
Nyctalus leisleri (Noctule de Leisler)	Rare, mostly in east	V
Nyctalus lasiopterus (Grande noctule)	Few isolated records	R
Miniopterus schreibersii (Minioptère)	Common in some parts of south	E
Plecotus auritus (Oreillard commun)	Fairly common and widespread	V
Plecotus austriacus (Oreillard méridional)	Fairly common everywhere	V
Barbastella barbastellus (Barbastelle)	Very rare, scattered records	E
Tadaria teniotis (Molosse de Cestoni)	Very rare, occurs only in south	R

Key And Protected Sites

A large number of caves in many parts of the country contain significant populations of bats. The largest colony in 'La grotte de Cabrespine' is a priority site for protection, but is threatened with development for tourism. It is likely other similar colonies may be found which, with others, will need to be protected by legal agreements as well as by grilles.

Tunnels, defence systems and crevices in walls and bridges, are all important for bat colonies and require protection and careful management.

Creation of New Roosts

There are many bat box schemes all over France and hibernation roosts are being installed in old military forts around Grenoble.

*Plate 14. Parti-coloured bat, **Vespertilio murinus**, is a highly migratory species spending the summer in northern Europe and flying south for winter. It is Europe's most colourful species and is often found in buildings in winter.*

Legislation

All bats were protected in 1981. It is forbidden to catch or kill bats without a licence, or to transport or sell them. However, bat roosts are not protected, nor is it an offence to disturb bats when they are roosting. These aspects should be covered by appropriate legislation. The National bat group has drawn up a code of conduct for its members, which seeks to prevent unnecessary disturbance to bats. It also seeks to ensure all research projects are necessary, of high quality and that reports are submitted annually to the Office for the Protection of Nature (Ministry of the Environment).

Education

Extensive publicity has been given in the media to the conservation needs of bats and detailing the work of the bat group. Books, booklets, posters, audio-visual and all types of educative materials have been produced and widely circulated. Being a large country, some areas of France have no bat specialists and a priority task, is to increase the number of members in the bat group.

Research

One of the most urgent requirements, is the study of food and feeding habitats of bats in various parts of the country. A two-year study is in progress, on the affects on bats of chemical timber treatments. It is hoped the use of these toxic chemicals may eventually be controlled throughout Europe. A long-term study is concerned with developing a monitoring programme for all species of bat, to enable a better understanding of the causes of changing status.

It is also hoped to study the incidence of the rabies-like virus in bats and its effect on populations, as well as assessing public opinion on this problem.

Bibliography

- Anon. (1984) *Atlas des mammifères sauvages de France.* Soc. Française. Étude. Protn. Mammifères. Paris.

- Brosset, A. (1978) Les Chauve-souris: disparaissent-elles? *Courrier Nature.* 55, 17-22.

- Noblet, J-F. (1986) Chauve-souris: les anges de la nuit. *Panda* (W.W.F.) Paris no. 27.

- Noblet, J-F., and Berthoud, G. (1985) *Les Chauve-souris de France, étude et protection.* FRAPNA édition Grenoble.

28

Switzerland and Liechstenstein

For many years, ornithologists setting nets in alpine passes to catch migrating birds, frequently caught bats. Some were already ringed showing they had flown over 700 kilometres from northern Europe, particularly from the Democratic Republic of Germany. After more than 30 years, similar discoveries continue to be made. However now there are many bat research, survey and conservation projects within Switzerland, which are co-ordinated from two centres in east and west Switzerland. In the east: Mr H.P. Stutz, FEBX, Singlistrasse 10, 8049 Zurich. In the west: Mr A Keller, Muséum Histoire Naturelle, C.P. 434, 1211 Genève 6.

Colonies of *Rhinolophus ferrumequinum* and *R. hipposideros*, especially in Valais, have shown such substantial declines that now they are close to extinction. Similar observations elsewhere suggest these and other cave dwelling species are greatly threatened.

Threats

Loss of roosts and overall change in agricultural practice have contributed most to observed reductions in bat populations. New, well insulated farm buildings of modern design are mostly unsuitable for bat roosts, and the demolition of old buildings is reducing the number of available sites. Intensification of agriculture in the lowlands (often involving the use of chemicals), has caused contraction in the area of 'waste' land, thereby reducing the abundance of flying insects.

Bats in hibernation, especially in caves, have been greatly disturbed, causing them to vacate roosts.

Bats of Switzerland and Liechstenstein and their Status

Scientific and Local Name	Frequency of Occurrence	Status
Rhinolophus ferrumequinum (Grosse Hufeisennase) Grand rhinolophe fer à cheval)	Fairly common especially in north	E
Rhinolophus hipposideros (Kleine Hufeisennase) (Petit rhinolophe fer à cheval)	Fairly rare throughout	E
Myotis mystacinus (Bartfledermaus) (Murin à moustaches)	Locally common, found everywhere	K
Myotis brandtii (Brandtfledermaus) (Vespertilion de Brandt)	Rare in north	R
Myotis emarginatus (Wimperfledermaus) (Murin à oreilles échancrées)	Rare, few records	I
Myotis daubentonii (Wasserfledermaus) (Murin de Daubenton)	Common everywhere	Nt
Myotis nattereri (Fransenfledermaus) (Murin de Natterer)	Very rare	K
Myotis bechsteinii (Bechsteinfledermaus) (Murin de Bechstein)	Rare, few scattered records, probably everywhere	K
Myotis myotis (Mausohr) (Grand murin)	Fairly common everywhere	V
Myotis blythi (Lkeines Mausohr) (Petit murin)	Rare, mostly south west	V
Pipistrellus pipistrellus (Zwergfledermaus) (Pipistrelle commune)	Common everywhere	Nt
Pipistrellus nathusii (Rauhhautfledermaus) (Pipistrelle de Nathusius)	Common in winter, migrates north in summer	Nt
Pipistrellus kuhli (Weissrandfledermaus) (Pipistrelle de Kuhl)	Rare in north, fairly common in south	I

Bats of Switzerland and Liechstenstein and their Status (continued)

Scientific and Local Name	Frequency of Occurrence	Status
Pipistrellus savii (Alpenfledermaus) Pipistrelle de Savi)	Fairly common in central Alps	R
Eptesicus serotinus (Breitflügelfledermaus) (Sérotine commune)	Fairly common, widespread	I
Eptesicus nilssonii (Nordfledermaus) (Sérotine de Nilsson)	Fairly abundant throughout	Nt
Vespertilio murinus (Zweifarbfledermaus) (Sérotine bicolor)	Possibly widespread, mostly migratory	K
Nyctalus noctula (Abendsegler) (Noctule commune)	Abundant throughout	Nt
Nyctalus leisleri (Kleinabendsegler) (Noctule de Leisler)	Fairly rare throughout	K
Nyctalus lasiopterus (Riesenabendsegler) (Noctule géante)	A few isolated records	K
Miniopterus schreibersii (Langflügelfledermaus) (Mioptère de Schreibers)	Fairly common in south west	E
Plecotus auritus (Braunes Langohr) (Oreillard commun)	Common throughout	Nt
Plectous austriacus (Graues Langohr) (Oreillard gris)	Common in lowland valleys, rare elsewhere	K
Barbastella barbastellus (Mopsfledermaus) (Barbastelle commune)	Very rare, few records	E
Tadarida teniotis (Bulldoggfledermaus) (Molosse de Cestoni)	Rare, southern Alps only	R

Felling old hollow trees used by bats for roosting, has probably become a serious problem for some species but observations are few. Large numbers of *Nyctalus noctula* are known to hibernate in rock crevices of precipices in the Jura, where climbers are known to cause disturbance and even death to some bats by driving pitons into the crevices. The number of bats affected is unknown. In some areas forests are dying as a result of air pollution. Although there may be some short-term advantage with the increase of insects living on dead wood, the long-term disadvantage is likely to be fewer insects and loss of potential roosting places.

Key and Protected Sites

The 'Cruex du Vent' Nature Reserve was extended to contain the most important cave colony of *Miniopterus schreibersii* and some of its feeding habitat. There are many other important roosts which need protection, particularly all the nurseries for the endangered species. Caves are especially important both as nursery sites and for hibernation. Some hibernation caves have already been protected with grilles, for example Grotte du chemin-de-fer, Neuchâtel, and Glitzersteinhöhle, Solothurn. Inventories of bat roosts are being compiled, from which the most important will need appropriate safeguards.

Conservation of Endangered Species

The causes of the substantial declines in the endangered species are not understood and research to investigate these is urgently needed. Research will be difficult on the rare *Barbastella barbastellus*, but *R. ferrumequinum* and *R. hipposideros* are still widespread. Attention should be focused on their ecological requirements as well as trying to identify causes of decline and continuing threats. Only as a result of this work can an adequate conservation plan be formulated.

Legislation

Bats were protected in Liechstenstein in 1933. In Switzerland, federal legislation protecting all bats was enacted in 1966, but some individual Cantons have been slow to introduce protective measures. The national legislation is difficult to interpret and no prosecutions have been taken. However, it seems likely breeding colonies in roofs are protected from wilful destruction, but not hibernation roosts. Since Switzerland has ratified the Bern

Convention, there is an obligation to ensure bats, their roosts and critical feeding habitat are afforded appropriate protection.

Education

A wide range of excellent educative material has been produced, including colour booklets and audio-visual packs describing the conservation requirements for bats. Although the bat group generates great media interest, its efforts are hampered to some extent by the lack of support from the national conservation agency. With the type of political structure which exists in Switzerland, it is difficult to see how an effective, wide ranging, co-ordinated conservation programme can be developed. Without unified action, adequate conservation will be achieved slowly.

To date, there has been no enforcement of the legislation. Little attempt has been made to implement the law, for instance by circulating information to appropriate people, or organisations, such as builders, architects and pest control companies. The bat group organises meetings and produces an annual bulletin 'Le Rhinolophe' to keep its members informed of conservation developments.

Research

Surveys should be continued and extended to find and subsequently monitor, roost sites. This is an essential requirement before value-judgements can be made as to which sites should be specially protected.

Annual monitoring of colonies is needed, to conform with similar studies in other European countries.

Bibliography

* Aellen, V. (1983) Migrations des chauves-souris en Suisse *Bonn. Zool. Beitr.* 34, 3-27.

* Apolhéloz, D., and Moeschler, P. (1987) L'enfant et la chauve-souris: enquête sur l'environnement psychologique des chiroptères. In *Des Animaux et des Hommes.* eds. J. Hainard and R. Kaehr. Musée d'ethnographie, Neuchâtel.

* Berthoud, G. (1986) *Protéger les chauves-souris dans les bâtiments.* Musée d'Histoire Naturelle, Genève.

* Gebhard, J. (1985) *Unsere Fledermaüse.* Naturhistorisches Museum, Basel. (also produced in French).

29
Italy

Recent observations by naturalists suggest bats are declining rapidly. Relatively few bats are now seen flying in large towns, but ten years ago it was common to see 'flocks' of hundreds of bats flying at sunset. Unfortunately, there is a lack of detailed information on the size of populations both in the past and at present, but it is likely that Italy once had very large colonies of several species.

There have been few studies of the distribution and abundance of the bats in Italy, but efforts are now being made to initiate and co-ordinate a research and conservation programme, through the development of a national bat group: Dr V. Calandra, Soc. Coop. Palma Nana, via Libertà, 95, Palermo.

Threats

Loss and damage to roosts appear to be the most serious problems, combined with the killing of bats when considered a nuisance. Bats living in historic buildings are often believed to cause damage to the structure and as a result they are killed. Similarly, colonies are excluded from many buildings because people fear them. Destruction of old buildings and walls, together with the felling of old hollow trees, is further reducing roosts.

Caves usually have uncontrolled access and many colonies have been driven away by disturbance, mainly due to tourist development and use as military stores.

Key And Protected Sites

No systematic survey has taken place to document and assess the conservation needs of bats in Italy. However, a few caves which

Italian Bats and their Status

Scientific and Local Name	Frequency of Occurrence	Status
Rhinolophus ferrumequinum (Ferro di cavello maggiore)	Fairly common everywhere	E
Rhinolophus hipposideros (Ferro de cavallo minore)	Fairly rare, widespread	E
Rhinolophus blasii (Ferro di cavallo di Blasius)	Rare in north east and Sicily, absent elsewhere	E
Rhinolophus euryale (Ferro di cavallo euryale)	Uncommon throughout	E
Rhinolophus mehelyi (Ferro di cavallo di Mehely)	Rare in south, absent elsewhere	E
Myotis mystacinus (Vespertilio mustacchino)	Rare throughout	V
Myotis emarginatus (Vespertilio emarginato)	Rare everywhere	E
Myotis capaccinii (Vespertilio di Capaccini)	Fairly common in south, absent in north	V
Myotis daubentonii (Vespertilio di Daubenton)	Fairly common and widespread	V
Myotis dasycneme (Vespertilio dasicneme)	Probably does not occur	--
Myotis nattereri (Vespertilio di Natterer)	Rare throughout, probably absent in Sardinia	V
Myotis bechsteinii (BVespertilio di Bechstein)	Few scattered records, mostly in north	R
Myotis myotis (Vespertilio maggiore)	Fairly common everywhere	V
Myotis blythi (Vespertilio di Blyth)	Fairly common everywhere	V
Pipistrellus pipistrellus (Pipistrello nano)	Very common throughout	Nt

Italian Bats and their Status (continued)

Scientific and Local Name	Frequency of Occurrence	Status
Pipistrellus nathusii (Pipistrello di Nathusius)	Rare throughout mainland	Nt
Pipistrellus kuhli (Pipistrello di Kuhl)	Fairly common throughout	V
Pipistrellus savii (Pipistrello di Savi)	Fairly common everywhere	V
Eptesicus serotinus (Serotino comune)	Fairly rare everywhere	K
Eptesicus nilssonii (Serotino di nilsson)	Very few records in north	I
Vespertilio murinus (Serotino bicolore)	Few records in north	I
Nyctalus noctula (Nottola comune)	Fairly rare throughout	V
Nyctalus leisleri (Nottola di Leisler)	Very few records	I
Nyctalus lasiopterus (Nottola gigante)	A few scattered records	I
Miniopterus schreibersii (Miniottero)	Common throughout	V or E
Plecotus auritus (Orecchione)	Fairly common in highlands and north	V
Plecotus austriacus (Orecchione meridionale)	Fairly common, probably occurs everywhere	V
Barbastella barbastellus (Barbastello)	Very rare, mostly in west	I
Tadarida teniotis (Molosso del Cestoni)	Fairly common everywhere	Nt

already are known to contain important colonies, are candidates for urgent protection. Undoubtedly, there are many thousands of caves which need investigation, but relatively few will have significant numbers of bats: in Veneto, Grotta della guerra, Grotta della Bislonga, Buco del Frate and Grotta a del Ponte di Veja; in Campania, Grotta di Castelcivita; in Ubruzzo, Grotta nera (which is already in the Fara S. Martino nature reserve); in Sicilia, Grotta dei Pipistrelli, Grotta dei Puntali, Duomo di Cefalù and Abbazia, Benedettina di S. Martino. Grotta nera and Grotta dei Pipistrelli are already protected with grilles at the entrance, but these and many more require full protection.

A few bat roosts have received a measure of protection because they are in areas of archaeological or palaeontological interest.

Legislation

Bats were legally protected in 1939, with further amendments in 1975, 1976 and 1980. However these laws are inadequate, partly because they do not protect the bats, their roosts or feeding habitat from deliberate disturbance, but also no implementation has occurred. Italy has ratified both the Bern and Bonn Conventions so there is an acknowledged responsibility to enact and implement protection for bats.

Education

The World Wildlife Fund (Italy) has been trying to establish a conservation and education programme for bats. This will be aided by the development of a national bat group. Most urgently needed is the production of leaflets and publicity material to initiate public education. To achieve this, the national authority responsible for nature conservation ought to provide some funding, because, as has happened in other countries, amateurs can provide a most cost-effective way of achieving the needs of bat conservation.

Research

There is an urgent need to survey and document bat roosts to enable sites to selected for protection. A number of these roosts should be monitored regularly in the recognised style adopted elsewhere in Europe. Funding is required if research is to be undertaken on the movements or migrations of bats, their food and feeding habitats.

Bibliography

- Crucitti, P., Bevilacqua, P., Daclon, C.M., Del Re, R. and Tringali, L. (1984) Progetto Bio Lazio. *Società Romana di Scienze Naturali*, Roma. 3-46.

- Pavan, M. (1985) *Appunti e documenti sulla situazione del patrimonio naturalistico Italiano.* Inst. Ento. Univ. Pavia. 83pp.

30
Austria

No account has been received.

The species composition and conservation problems are similar to those in Switzerland and the southern part of the Federal Republic of Germany.

Bats are legally protected. The first legislation, dates from 1907 but was improved in 1939.

31
Hungary

No recent report was received.

A few scientists have studied various aspects of the bats of Hungary, especially since the 1950s. This involved detailed research on systematics, activity periods of various species throughout the night, as well as elucidating the criteria bats appear to adopt for their roost selection. Also important sub-fossil cave deposits have shown the changing distribution of species with time. Some of the present-day African species lived in Hungary in the inter-glacial periods.

However, modern studies have shown many species have suffered substantial declines in abundance since the 1950s. Renovation of historic buildings including churches, combined with the development of modern agriculture are thought to have caused some of the decline. Scientific research which involved ringing bats is known to have contributed significantly to some declines, especial-ly of *Rhinolophus ferrumequinum* which is particularly sensitive to poorly designed and manufactured rings.

Legislation

Bats were first protected in 1901, with amendments to the legisla-tion in 1954, 1974 and 1975. These Decrees gave protection to bats, but their roosts and habitats are not safeguarded. There has been no implementation of the laws and generally people are un-aware of the needs for bat conservation.

Hungary has ratified the Bonn Convention, therefore the State clearly recognises the need for adequate conservation measures.

Hungarian Bats and their Status

Scientific and Local Name	Frequency of Occurrence	Status
Rhinolophus ferrumequinum (Nagy patkósdenevér)	Fairly rare, widespread	E
Rhinolophus hipposideros (Kis patkósdenevér)	Fairly rare	E
Rhinolophus euryale (Kereknyergü patkósdenevér)	Very rare, occurs only in east	E
Myotis mystacinus (Bajuszos denevér)	Rare throughout	V
Myotis brandtii (Brandts denevér)	Very rare, only in north	V
Myotis emarginatus (Csonkafülü denevér)	Very rare everywhere	E
Myotis daubentonii (Vizi denevér)	Fairly common everywhere	Nt
Myotis dasycneme (Tavi denevér)	Few scattered records	I
Myotis nattereri (Horgasszörü denevér)	Uncommon everywhere	V
Myotis bechsteinii (Nagyfülü denevér)	Rare throughout	R
Myotis myotis (Közömséges denevér)	Fairly common everywhere	V?E
Myotis blythi	Rare throughout	V
Pipistrellus pipistrellus (Törpe denevér)	Very common everywhere	Nt
Pipistrellus nathusii (Durvavitorlájú denevér)	Fairly rare throughout	R
Eptesicus serotinus (Kései denevér)	Fairly common everywhere	Nt

Hungarian Bats and their Status (continued)

Scientific and Local Name	Frequency of Occurrence	Status
Eptesicus nilssonii (Nilsson denevér)	Few records in east	R
Vespertilio murinus (Fehértorkü denevér)	Scattered records throughout	R
Nyctalus noctula (Korai denevér)	Common everywhere	Nt
Nyctalus leisleri (Szöröskarú denevér)	Rare throughout	R
Nyctalus lasiopterus (Nagy korai denevér)	A few records including breeding	I
Miniopterus schreibersii (Hosszuszárnyú denevér)	Rare, almost everywhere	V
Plecotus auritus (Hosszüfülü denevér)	Rare throughout	E
Plecotus austriacus (Ösz hosszüfülü denevér)	Fairly common everywhere	V
Barbastella barbastellus (Pisze denevér)	Rare everywhere	R

A priority is to produce and circulate educative materials, followed by documentation and protection of important roosts and foraging habitat.

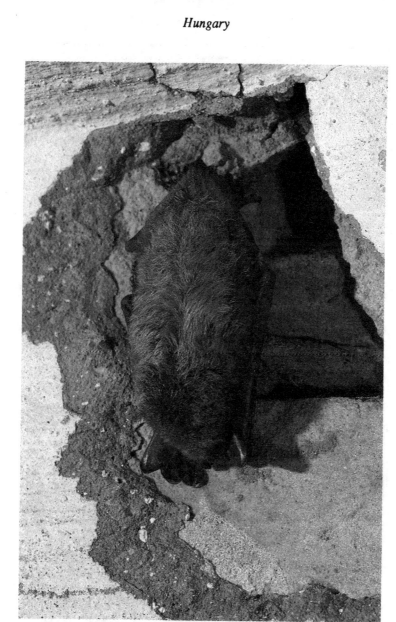

Plate 15. The pond bat, **Myotis dasycneme**, is perhaps Europe's most endangered species, found primarily in the north west of the Netherlands and Denmark. Many colonies have been poisoned by timber treatments in buildings.

32
Yugoslavia

The internationally known, spectacular tourist caves of Skocjanske Jame and Postojnska Jame have long been known to shelter large numbers of bats. However, within Yugoslavia there are several tens of thousands of caves, many of which probably contain significant numbers of bats. A large number of caves are known to have been filled in with domestic rubbish, while bats in others were over-disturbed or killed. A few biologists have done some research on various aspects of the distribution and biology of their bats, but Yugoslavia has been a popular place to visit for foreign

*Plate 16. Nathusius' pipistrelle, **Pipistrellus nathusii**, one of the most migratory of species, flying from Estonia and Lithuania SSR's to Western European coasts, especially the Netherlands. Other specimens fly south to winter near the Mediterranean.*

Bats of Yugoslavia and their Status

Scientific and Local Name	Frequency of Occurrence	Status
Rhinolophus ferrumequinum (Veliki potkovicar)[1] (Veliki podkovnjak)[2]	Fairly common everywhere	V
Rhinolophus hipposideros (Mali potcovicar)[1] (Mali podkovnjak)[2]	Uncommon everywhere	E
Rhinolophus blasii (Sredozemni potkovicar)[1] (Blazijev podkovnjak)[2]	Rare, occurs near coast only	V
Rhinolophus euryale (Juzni potkovicar)[1] (Juzni podkovnjak)[2]	Very rare, occurs west and south	E
Rhinolophus mehelyi (Meheljev potkovicar)[1] (Meheljev podkovnjak)[2]	Very rare, coastal	V
Myotis mystacinus (Brkati sismis)[1] (Brkati netopir)[2]	Uncommon, widespread	V
Myotis emarginatus (Trobojni sismis)[1] (Vejicati netopir)[2]	Uncommon, widespread	V
Myotis capaccinii (Dugonogi sismis)[1] (Dolgonogi netopir)[2]	Rare, occurs in west and south	V
Myotis daubentonii (Povodni sismis)[1] (Obvodni netopir)[2]	Very rare, few scattered records	R
Myotis dasycneme (Pobarski sismis)[1] (Mocvirski netopir)[2]	Two records only	Ex
Myotis nattereri (Rojtasti sismis)[1] (Resasti netopir)[2]	Very rare, mostly west and north	R

Bats of Yugoslavia and their Status

Scientific and Local Name	Frequency of Occurrence	Status
Myotis bechsteinii (Dugouhi sismis)[1] Velikouhi netopir)[2]	Few scattered records in north	K
Myotis myotis (Veliki sismis)[1] (Navadni netopir)[2]	Uncommon, widespread	E
Myotis blythi (Ostrouhi sismis)[1] (Ostrouhi netopir)[2]	Rare in north, more common near coast	E
Pipistrellus pipistrellus (Patuljasti netopir)[1] (Mali netopir)[2]	Common everywhere	Nt
Pipistrellus nathusii (Natuzijusov netopir)[1] (Crnoprogi netopir)[2]	Rare, widespread	V
Pipistrellus kuhli (Belorubi netopir)[1] (Belorubi netopir)[2]	Fairly common near coast, absent elsewhere	Nt
Pipistrellus savii (Savijev netopir)[1] (Alpinski netopir)[2]	Common on coast, rare or absent elsewhere	Nt
Eptesicus serotinus (Veliki nocnik)[1] (Sirokokrili netopir)[2]	Uncommon but widespread	V
Eptesicus nilssonii (Severni nocnik)[1] (Severni netopir)[2]	Two records only	K
Vespertilio murinus (Dvobojni ljiljak)[1] (Ponocni netopir, Dvobarvni netopir)[2]	Rare, probably widespread	V
Nyctalus noctula (Rani vecernik)[1] (Navadni mracnik)[2]	Fairly common and widespread	V

Bats of Yugoslavia and their Status (continued)

Scientific and Local Name	Frequency of Occurrence	Status
Nyctalus leisleri (Mali vecernik)[1] (Gozdni mracnik)[2]	Very rare, only four coastal records	K
Nyctalus lasiopterus (Dzinovski vecernik)[1] (Veliki mracnik)[2]	Very rare, few coastal records	K
Miniopterus schreibersii (Dugokrili krilas)[1] (Dolgokrili netopir)[2]	Common, widespread	E
Plecotus auritus (Mrki dugousan)[1] (Rjavi uhati netopir)[2]	Rare, mostly in highlands in north	V
Plecotus austriacus (Sivi dugousan)[1] (Sivi uhati netopir)[2]	Fairly rare, widespread	V
Barbastella barbastellus (Crni sirokousan)[1] (Sirokouhi netopir)[2]	Very rare, occurs only in north	V
Tadarida teniotis (Sirokouhi golorepas)[1] (Dolgorepi netopir)[2]	Rare, south and west coast only	V

1 - Serbo-Croatian; 2 - Slovenian

scientists for short duration studies. Unfortunately bats are not popular and few people have shown an interest in their study or conservation. The collator of conservation information is Professor B. Dulíc, Department of Zoology, Rooseveltov trg 6, 41000 Zagreb.

Threats

Destruction of caves and disturbance of roosts are both serious problems affecting many sites. However, perhaps more serious is the large number of bats of many species which are killed each year. Several colonies of *Rhinolophus hipposideros* in buildings, have been killed, sometimes by children using air guns, as well as colonies of *Myotis myotis, Nyctalus noctula* and *Pipistrellus pipistrellus.* This destruction often occurs in winter, when it is likely some bats will have migrated from countries further north.

All the *Rhinolophus* spp. frequently are killed in caves, as well as numerous *M. myotis, M. blythi* and *Miniopterus schreibersii.* Since these latter species especially tend to be migratory, efforts must be made to stop such destruction of colonies.

Key Sites

Relatively few caves have been surveyed of the thousands existing in the country and no attempt has been made to produce a comprehensive dossier listing important sites. This is a huge task, but one which is urgently required.

Caves and buildings are known to contain important roosts. About 1,000 *R. ferrumequinum* breed in a building in the Voivodinia region and nearby, another building houses a nursery colony of 200 to 300 *M. emarginatus.* A few caves which contain large colonies, especially of *M. schreibersii,* already have some protection as tourist sites, but generally bat numbers have probably declined due to the lighting and other disturbance.

Legislation and Education

Bats were given National protection in 1947, but there has been no attempt at implementation either at State level or of the individual Federated Socialist Republics, which comprise Yugoslavia. Interested biologists have for many years tried to persuade the authorities in a number of the Republics to produce and circulate information about bats. Some private attempts to protect sites have been fruitless. Because of the importance of the Yugoslavian bat fauna in the European context, it is most important to have adequate legislation, suitably implemented. Clearly, lack of finance has hampered the willing efforts of the biologists, but with some support, for the production and circulation of educative materials combined with active protection of vital sites, much could be achieved relatively quickly.

Bibliography

- Dulic, B. (1988) Bats in the Red Data Book of Croatia. *Proc. 4th Bat Research Symposium, Prague (1987).*

* Krystufek, B. (1988) Distribution of bats in Slovenia, Yugoslavia. *Proc. 4th Bat Research Symposium, Prague (1987).*

33
Romania

No recent report was received.

There have been few studies of any aspects of the Romanian bat fauna. However, it is known that in the past there were some large cave bat populations in the Dobrogea coastal region. These have declined considerably. For instance in the cave 'Pestera Liliecilor de la Gura Dobrogei' a nursery colony of *Rhinolophus mehelyi* numbered about 500 in 1974, but only 100 to 150 bats remained in 1979. The same cave sheltered a breeding colony of *Myotis blythi* in 1974, which totalled 4,000 to 5,000 bats but only 150 to 200 survived in 1979. At the same time this cave also supported up to 3,000 *Miniopterus schreibersii*, but less than 200 were there in 1979. Overall this represents a population decline of nearly 94 per cent in five years.

It is not known what caused this dramatic decline, but the caves are internationally known and are frequently visited by Romanians and foreign tourists.

Another cave in the same area 'Pestera de la Gura Dobrogei' was known to have hibernating clusters of *Pipistrellus pipistrellus*, estimated to contain up to 100,000 bats in the mid 1950s. However, recent reports suggest these too, have declined substantially.

Legislation

It is not clear whether bats are fully protected in Romania. It appears some protection was afforded in 1973 but nothing is known as to whether implementation has occurred or whether any educative materials have been produced and circulated.

Bibliography

- Barbu, P. (1974) Ocrotirea liliecilor. *Ocrot. nat.* 18, 29-36.
- Cerveny, J. (1982) Notes on the bat fauna (Chiroptera) of Roumanian Dobrogea. *Nyctalus* (NF). 1, 349-357.

34
Bulgaria

No recent report was received.

There have been a number of research studies of the distribution of bats in Bulgaria. Some large colonies are found in caves. One such cave 'Uruska maara' in Lovec, contained about 10,000 hibernating bats, mostly a mixture of *Myotis myotis, M. blythi* and *Miniopterus schreibersii*. Another cave 'Prilepnata pestera' in Vraca district, sheltered about 5,000 bats of the same species together with some *M. capaccinii*.

Undoubtedly there are many other very important roosts, most of which will need protection.

Legislation

Wildlife legislation was enacted in 1962, which protected bats and all cave dwelling animals. Therefore, it is assumed cave roosts are fully protected. It is not known whether the legislation has been implemented.

Bibliography

* Beron, P. (1961) Contribution à la connaissance des chauves-souris Bulgares. *Fragmenta Balcanica*. 3, 189-194.

35
Greece

There have been few attempts to document the Greek bat fauna and little is known about the status of each species. A small number of biologists have sporadically listed small collections of bats often caught in restricted areas, but population counts are lacking. About 25 species have been recorded (24 are known residents), but almost certainly a further three or four species are likely to occur. Because of the variety of habitats and the position of the country with many thousands of caves, Greece is likely to have particularly important and unique associations of bat fauna. Documenting this is a vital and urgent need. Two people are concerned about the conservation status of bats. On the mainland: Dr J.G. Iliopoulou-Georgudaki, Faculty of Science, University of Patras, Patra, and on Crete: Dr A. Legakis, Department of Biology, P O Box 1470, 71110 Iraklion.

Although there are no quantitative results, biologists since the early 1970s have observed a remarkable decline in numbers of bats, especially of the cave and tree dwelling species. This reduction has been particularly severe near olive plantations.

Threats

The most important roosts are caves of which, more than 8,000 are known and some used to contain very large bat colonies. Caves are used for religious ceremonies, for sheltering livestock such as sheep or goats or for developing tourism, all of which drive bats away.

Greek Bats and their Status

Scientific and Local Name	Frequency of Occurrence	Status
Rhinolophus ferrumequinum (Rhinolophos i megali)	Fairly common everywhere	V
Rhinolophus hipposideros (Rhinolophos i mikra)	Fairly rare	V
Rhinolophus blasii (Rhinolophos i Blasios)	Rare throughout	R
Rhinolophus euryale (Rhinolophos i mesogiaki)	Very rare throughout	R
Rhinolophus mehelyi (Rhinolophos i Mehelios)	Very rare throughout	R
Myotis mystacinus (Nycteris i mystakophoros)	Very rare throughout	R
Myotis emarginatus (Nycteris i blephardoti)	Very rare throughout	R
Myotis capaccinii (Nycteris i macropus)	Rare but widespread	R
Myotis nattereri (Nycteris i Krossoti)	Very rare, occurs in north west	I
Myotis myotis (Nycteris i pontikootos)	Fairly rare throughout	R
Myotis blythi (Nycteris i oxygnathos)	Fairly common throughout	V
Pipistrellus pipistrellus (Nycteris i kini)	Fairly rare throughout	R
Pipistrellus nathusii (Nycteris i trachydermos)	Very rare throughout	R
Pipistrellus kuhli (Nycteris i leukogyros)	Very common, absent in north east	Nt
Pipistrellus savii (Nycteris i alpios)	Rare everywhere	R

Greek Bats and their Status (continued)

Scientific and Local Name	Frequency of Occurrence	Status
Eptesicus serotinus (Nycteris i eurypteryx)	Rare throughout	R
Vespertilio murinus (Nycteris i dichromos)	Rare throughout	R
Nyctalus noctula (Nycteris pterygisti i esperobios)	Rare everywhere	R
Nyctalus leisleri (Nycteris pterygisti i mikra)	Very rare, only a few records	R
Nyctalus lasiopterus (Nycteris pterygisti i megali)	A few scattered records	--
Miniopterus schreibersii (Nycteris i macropterys)	Common everywhere	V
Plecotus auritus (Nycteris makrootos i europaiki)	Rare, only in north east	R
Plecotus austriacus (Nycteris makrootos i mesogiaki)	Rare, widespread	R
Tadarida teniotis (Nycteris i urophoros)	Rare everywhere	R

But worst of all is the deliberate fumigation of caves to kill bats. This is commonly done in summer, sometimes just for 'fun', but also because shepherds and other local people fear the bats.

There is extensive use of agricultural pesticides and it is believed regular large scale aerial spraying of olive plantations, has caused some of the observed reductions in numbers of bats.

Forests, especially in the central and northern areas, are being felled and an increasing incidence of destruction of others by summer fires is both destroying roosts and depriving bats of one of their major feeding habitats.

*Plate 17. Serotine, **Eptesicus serotinus**, one of the most common species in the extreme north west of Europe, where it may be expanding its range.*

Key Sites

Because of the lack of any detailed knowledge, it is not possible to list any special sites. However, caves represent the most important roost resource in which the largest aggregations of bats are found. Many of these will need protection.

Legislation

Bats were given protection in a number of Decrees from 1969 to 1980. It is forbidden to catch, kill, sell or transport bats or to own them, but licences can be issued to allow scientific research or collecting for museums. Bat roosts are not protected unless they are within national parks or hunting reserves.

No attempt has been made to implement this legislation and the public are unaware of the need for bat conservation. In fact, the public are hostile to bats and generally kill them when they are found.

Education

No leaflets or other educative material have been produced. These are urgently needed together with resources to begin a wide ranging education programme, from school children to all sections of the community, including those who visit caves such as speolologists and particularly tourist guides.

The Greek government has ratified the Bern Convention and therefore has recognised its obligations to begin an effective conservation programme for bats. The resources needed to initiate this need not be large if the country's present expertise is utilised effectively. Education is the most urgent priority.

Research

The second priority is to survey and document roosts and to begin a programme of site protection. There is sufficient expertise amongst the University-based scientists to organise such surveys, but funding is required for staff and transport.

36
Albania

No information was received from Albania.

The species composition will be similar to those of Yugoslavia and Greece, as will be the conservation problems. However, the agricultural and technological development in Albania is less than surrounding countries and consequently, their bats may be surviving better. Undoubtedly some bats will migrate between these States.

It is not known whether bats are protected, nor whether there are any conservation measures for them.

37
Malta

There have been few reliable studies of the bats living in Malta. Therefore, it is not known which species are resident nor whether migrants regularly occur. At least 14 species have been reported, but probably no more than five are resident and only two are abundant. Identification is doubtful for several species.

A recent developing interest in bats is focussing attention on the need to conserve Maltese species. The co-ordinator is Mr J. Borg, Block C2/5 Housing Estate, Ta'Xbiex.

Threats

Maltese bats live mostly in caves and these have been threatened by disturbance and vandalistic killing. Early in 1987, about 100 hibernating bats, thought to be *Myotis blythi*, were deliberately killed when a fire was lit beneath them. Similar destruction has occurred in the past. Caves are being destroyed by vandalism and by urbanisation when entrances are closed prior to building developments. The largest known breeding colony on the islands for *M. blythi* occurs in the cave 'Ghar il-Friefet', and this was threatened with such development in 1984. Destruction of this vital site was prevented by a well supported public protest.

Key Sites

Three caves are regarded as important for the Maltese bats. 'Ghar il-Friefet' contains a nursery colony of about 200 *M. blythi*, but the bats do not remain in winter.

Bats of Malta and their Status

Scientific and Local Name	Frequency of Occurrence	Status
Rhinolophus hipposideros* Farfett il-lejl Tan-Nala zghir)	Very rare	I
Myotis myotis (Farfett il-lejl Widnet il-Gurdien Kbir)	Possibly a vagrant	K
Myotis blythi* (Farfett il-lejl Widnet il-Gurdien Zghir)	Fairly common	V
Pipistrellus pipistrellus* (Pipistrell)	Common	V
Pipistrellus kuhli (Pipistrell ta'Kuhl)	Possibly rare	K
Miniopterus schreibersii (Farfett il-lejl ta'Xrajber)	Possibly a vagrant	K
Plecotus austriacus* (Farfett il-lejl ta' Widnejh Kbar)	Rare	V

*Known resident species.

'Gar Hassan' often shelters up to 100 *M. blythi* and a few *Plecotus austriacus*, but mostly in the autumn. Girgenti's Cave usually has up to 50 *M. blythi* in winter with some *Rhinolophus hipposideros*.

Undoubtedly other caves will contain significant numbers of bats, but being relatively small islands (320 square kilometres), it is possible there is but a single colony of *M. blythi* which seasonally occupies many sites. None of these caves is protected and the second site is already being degraded, as it is visited as a tourist attraction.

Legislation

Bats are not protected. It is essential that legislation should be enacted to protect the islands fragile wildlife resources. Many local naturalists are concerned about their heritage and with a little financial support an adequate education programme could be effected. This, together with site surveys will enable selection of those roosts which need protection.

Part Three

Species Accounts

Species Accounts

Brief accounts are given for each of the 30 species of bat in
Europe. Space only allows a general indication to be given of requirements for roosts, habitat and food. The various species may
have life-styles which differ over their range. For example, *P.
pipistrellus* in north west Europe roosts mostly in buildings and is
not usually found in caves, whereas in south eastern Europe, dense
clusters occur in caves.

Maps

These show the overall distribution of each species. The maps
will be inaccurate for several reasons. Firstly, there has been
little detailed study of species distribution over most of the land
surface, and some species are hard to find.

Secondly, the maps do not show relative abundance of a species
across its range, so some large areas depicted as the species
range, in reality depend on a small number of isolated records,
while in other areas bats are very common. Bats are highly
mobile and capable of covering long distances quickly, therefore
it is not unreasonable to estimate 30 kilometres radii around each
positive identification to show where the species may occur. In
some relatively small areas, comprehensive searches have been
completed using bat detectors, which have produced a clearer picture of bat distribution. In time, detailed studies of one species
living in a mountainous country may show it mostly lives in certain types of habitat such as lowland agricultural valleys. It may
never go over the mountains but the maps presented here aim to

show the overall range rather than the detail. They complement the species list in each country account.

Thirdly, the range and abundance of each species may be changing, and some distributional information is based on records from 50 years or more ago.

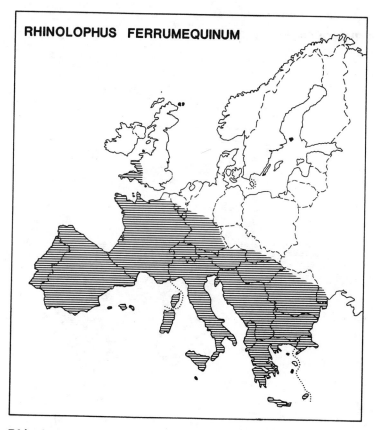

RHINOLOPHUS FERRUMEQUINUM

Rhinolophus ferrumequinum - **Schreber 1774**

Size
Forearm length: 51-61mm, Wingspan: 350-400mm, Body mass: 14-34g

Distribution
Occurs in the entire Palaearctic from Britain to Japan

Habitat
Mostly cave dwelling but has adapted to larger buildings for nurseries especially in northern Europe. Associated with mixture of pasture, scrub and woodland.

Status
Populations greatly reduced in most areas. Now regarded as endangered.

RHINOLOPHUS HIPPOSIDEROS

Rhinolophus hipposideros - **Bechstein 1800**

Size	Forearm length: 35-42.5mm, Wingspan: 200-250mm, Body mass: 4-9g
Distribution	From Ireland to Kashmir and Poland to north Africa
Habitat	Nurseries found predominantly in warm caves in southern areas but roofs of buildings mostly used in the north. Hibernates in caves, mines and cellars usually close to the nursery.
Status	Locally extinct in some northern areas with populations generally in decline. Regarded as endangered in many regions.

RHINOLOPHUS BLASII

Rhinolophus blasii - **Peters 1886**

Size   Forearm length: 45-50mm, Wingspan: 260-310
                  mm, Body mass: 11-16g.

Distribution Occurs from Italy and south east Europe, Morocco
                  and Tunisia east to Afghanistan.

Habitat   Nurseries in caves and mines where large clusters
                  are found. These sites are generally in well
                  vegetated areas but may be found in open and
                  scrub habitats.

Status   Little known and possibly overlooked species.
                  Threatened by disturbance and destruction in
                  caves.

RHINOLOPHUS EURYALE

Rhinolophus euryale - **Blasius 1853.**

Size	Forearm length: 42-50mm, Wingspan: 290-325mm, Body mass: 10-18g.
Distribution	Found widely throughout southern Europe including the large islands and east to Iran.
Habitat	Roosts in caves throughout the year where large nurseries may be mixed with other *Rhinolophus* spp. Mostly found in well wooded country close to water.
Status	A vulnerable species which is declining in some areas, due partly to disturbance in caves.

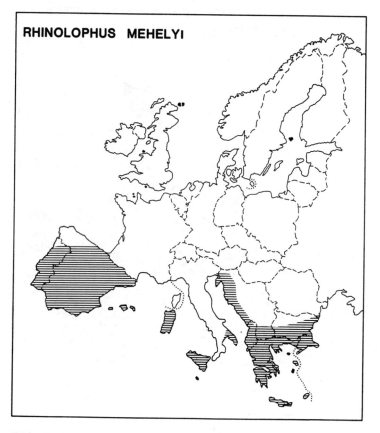

RHINOLOPHUS MEHELYI

Rhinolophus mehelyi - **Matschie 1901.**

Size Forearm length: 48-55mm, Wingspan: 320-360mm, Body mass: 12-20g.

Distribution Occurs patchily in southern Europe and Mediterranean islands, north west Africa and east to Iran.

Habitat Roosts in caves throughout the year, often associated with other *Rhinolophus* spp, *M. myotis* and *Miniopterus schreibersii*.

Status Rare and may be declining rapidly through disturbance and loss of caves.

Myotis mystacinus - **Kuhl 1819.**

Size	Forearm length: 30-37mm, Wingspan: 200-240mm, Body mass: 4-8g.
Distribution	Found throughout Palaearctic from Ireland to Japan.
Habitat	In summer, nursery colonies mostly found in buildings but occur in trees and exceptionally in tunnels. Hibernates in caves, mines and cellars. Feeds around woodland and in riparian habitats.
Status	Some populations are in decline. Appears to be most threatened by remedial timber treatment.

Myotis brandtii - **Eversmann 1845**

Size	Forearm length: 31-39mm, Wingspan: 200-255mm, Body mass: 4-10g.
Distribution	First recognised in 1971, it appears to be restricted to central and northern Europe.
Habitat	Summer roosts mostly in buildings but also occur in trees. Hibernates in caves and mines. Generally found around woodlands in agricultural and other rural areas.
Status	Little known about the status of this widespread species, but chemical timber treatments are known to have killed some colonies.

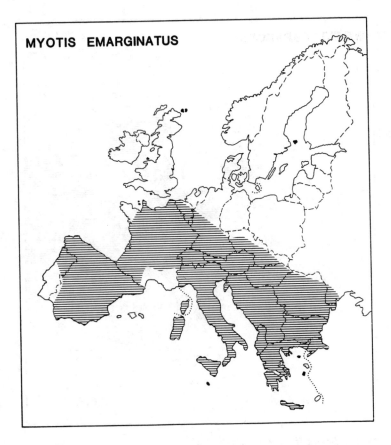

MYOTIS EMARGINATUS

Myotis emarginatus - **Geoffroy 1806.**

Size	Forearm length: 36-42mm, Wingspan: 220-250mm, Body mass: 6-14g.
Distribution	Central and southern Europe but reaches the Netherlands and Poland, north Africa and Iran.
Habitat	Nurseries occur in caves, trees and buildings. Mostly hibernates in warm caves, mines and cellars. Prefers to feed in parkland with mixture of pasture, marshland and open water.
Status	Endangered species, already virtually extinct in some northern areas. Disturbance in caves has caused some decline.

Myotis capaccinii - **Bonaparte 1837**

Size	Forearm length: 38-44mm, Wingspan: 230-290mm, Body mass: 6-15g.
Distribution	Found in Mediterranean areas from Spain to Bulgaria and Greece.
Habitat	Roosts in caves throughout the year often with *Rhinolophus* spp. and other *Myotis* bats. Feeds in riparian woodland and scrubby areas.
Status	Possibly a relict species. Appears to be rare and declining but requires careful study.

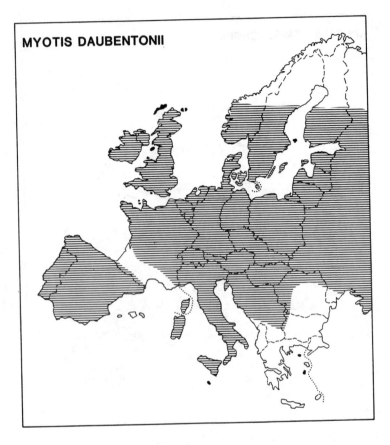

MYOTIS DAUBENTONII

Myotis daubentonii - **Kuhl 1819**

Size   Forearm length: 33-41mm, Wingspan: 230-275mm,
                Body mass: 6-12g.

Distribution   Throughout Europe (except extreme north) east to
                Japan. Absent from southern Palaearctic.

Habitat   Nurseries occur in wide variety of places from cool
                damp tunnels to warm dry roof spaces, where bats
                may mix with other species. Feeds mostly in
                riparian habitat, often over water.

Status   Some local populations in central and northern
                Europe have increased substantially, while others
                have declined. Major threat is loss of roosts in walls.

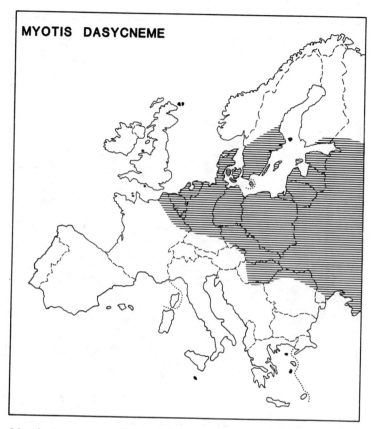

MYOTIS DASYCNEME

Myotis dasycneme - **Boie 1825.**

Size	Forearm length: 43-50mm, Wingspan: 250-325mm, Body mass: 14-22g.
Distribution	Three main centres, Netherlands to Denmark, around Leningrad and southern Urals, but scattered through central and eastern Europe.
Habitat	Nurseries found mostly in large roof spaces close to water over which they feed. Hibernates in caves, cellars and mines.
Status	An endangered species which has declined substantially in all major centres, due to remedial timber treatments and pollution of waterways.

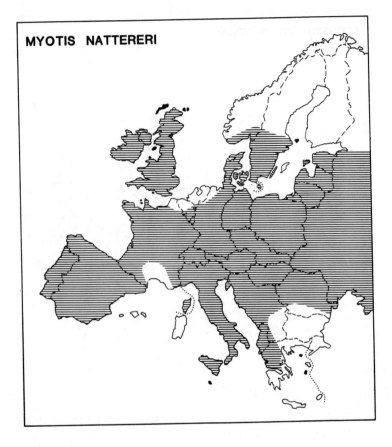

MYOTIS NATTERERI

Myotis nattereri - **Kuhl 1818.**

Size	Forearm length: 36-43mm, Wingspan: 240-300mm, Body mass: 6-12g.
Distribution	Throughout most of Europe, north Africa and east to Japan.
Habitat	In summer, roosts mostly in buildings and hollow trees but nurseries also found in caves and mines. Latter are major hibernation sites. Feeds along forest edges, often close to water.
Status	Some large declines are reported, especially from colonies subjected to remedial timber treatment.

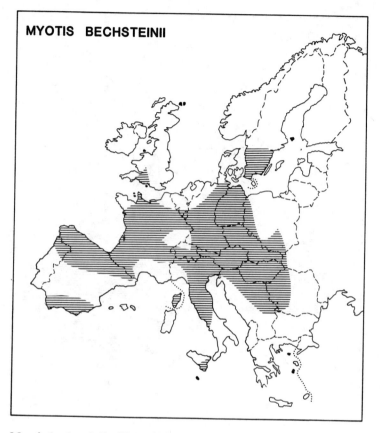

Myotis bechsteinii - **Kuhl 1818.**

Size   Forearm length: 38-47mm, Wingspan: 250-300mm,
                  Body mass 7-13g.

Distribution Much of Europe from Spain and France, to the
                  Ukraine and Caucasus.

Habitat   Nursery colonies occur in trees, but also roosts in
                  buildings. Uses caves in winter. Requires extensive
                  woodland and parkland where it feeds amongst
                  vegetation.

Status   Very rare everywhere. Possibly declining due to
                  loss of forest and climatic change.

Myotis myotis - **Borkhausen 1797.**

Size	Forearm length: 56-68mm, Wingspan: 350-450mm, Body mass: 27-45g.
Distribution	Most of Europe including Mediterranean islands east to Palestine, but excluding Scandanavia and the British Isles.
Habitat	Often roosts in caves and mines throughout the year in large clusters. Also has nurseries in roofs and trees. Feeds in open woodland and over pasture sometimes near to urban developments.
Status	Extinction of colonies and declines over much of Europe have resulted in 'endangered' designation.

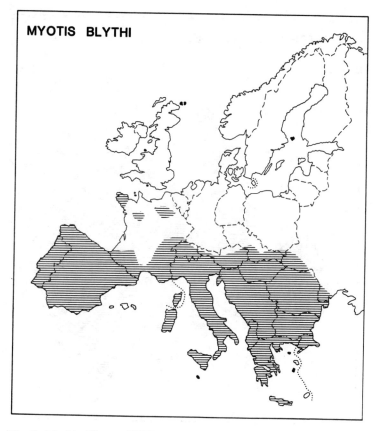

Myotis blythi - **Tomes 1857.**

Size	Forearm length: 50-60mm, Wingspan: 370-410mm, Body mass: 15-32g.
Distribution	Southern Europe and most Mediterranean islands, north west Africa, east to Himalayas.
Habitat	Mostly lives in caves throughout the year but in northern parts uses buildings. Also found in trees. Feeds in woods, parkland and at edge of rural areas.
Status	Regarded as endangered because of the loss and decline of colonies caused largely by disturbance and killing.

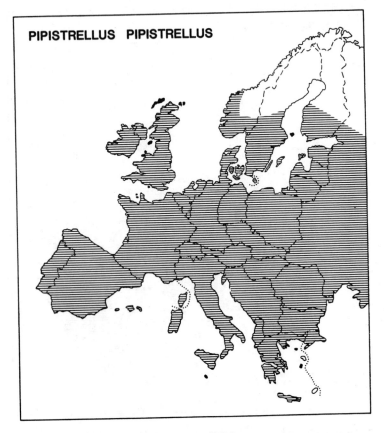

Pipistrellus pipistrellus - **Schreber 1774.**

Size Forearm length: 28-35mm, Wingspan: 180-250mm, Body mass: 4-9g.

Distribution Almost all Europe east to Afghanistan and including north and west Africa.

Habitat Roosts predominantly in buildings throughout the year, but also hibernates in caves in southern and eastern Europe. An urban bat, feeds in agricultural and lightly wooded areas.

Status Many large colonies have disappeared or been killed. Agricultural and timber treatment chemicals have killed many bats.

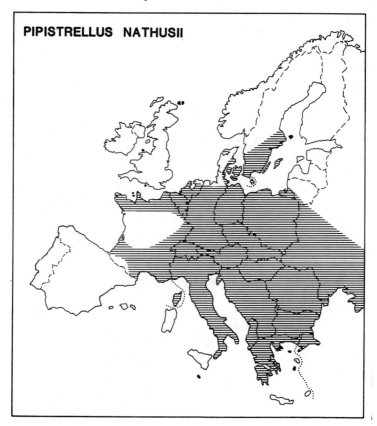

PIPISTRELLUS NATHUSII

Note: Widespread in eastern Baltic states to 61°N (S. Finland)

Pipistrellus nathusii - **Keyserling & Blasius 1839.**

Size   Forearm length: 32-37mm, Wingspan: 220-255mm, Body mass: 5-10g.

Distribution Western Europe (excluding Spain and British Isles) to Urals and Caucasus. May be spreading west.

Habitat   Roosts in buildings and trees throughout year and often in bat boxes. Prefers riparian habitats for feeding but found in urban parkland and woodland. Sometimes found with *Myotis* spp.

Status   Increasing in abundance in western areas, but little is known.

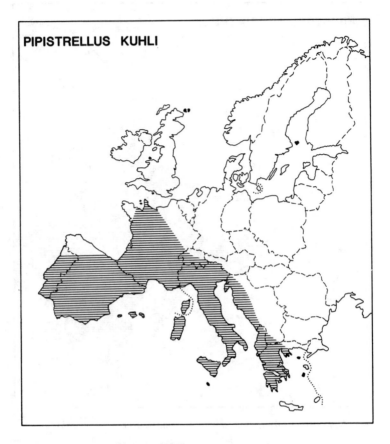

Pipistrellus kuhli - **Kuhl 1819.**

Size	Forearm length: 31-36mm, Wingspan: 210-250mm, Body mass: 5-9g.
Distribution	South and west Europe to Pakistan and south west Asia. Also occurs in much of Africa.
Habitat	Principal roosts in buildings but also found in trees, bat boxes and walls. Feeds in urban and agricultural areas.
Status	Little known. Appears to have been overlooked, as suggested by new records in northern France.

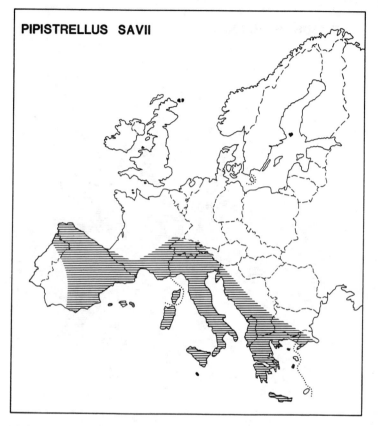

PIPISTRELLUS SAVII

Pipistrellus savii - **Bonaparte 1837.**

Size	Forearm length: 31-37mm, Wingspan: 210-255mm, Body mass: 5-10g.
Distribution	Areas bordering Mediterranean, including Canary and Cape Verde Islands, and north east Africa east to Japan.
Habitat	Roosts predominantly in caves, rock crevices and buildings, mostly in mountainous regions. Feeds in and around woodland
Status	Very little known, but is threatened by remedial timber treatment.

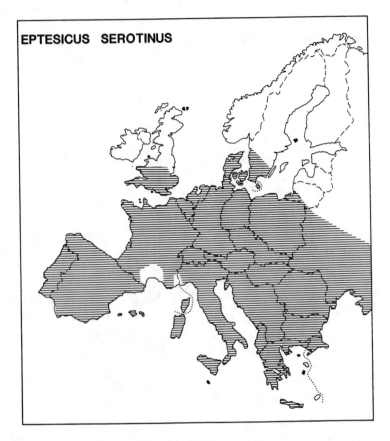

EPTESICUS SEROTINUS

Eptesicus serotinus - **Schreber 1774.**

Size	Forearm length: 48-56mm, Wingspan: 330-380mm, Body mass: 15-35g.
Distribution	From western Europe and north Africa (excluding northern areas) east to Korea.
Habitat	Nurseries mostly in buildings but occasionally found in hollow trees. Hibernates in same roosts as summer, also in crevices in caves in east and north. Feeds in sheltered urban areas.
Status	Common over large areas and possibly spreading north. Some colonies have declined.

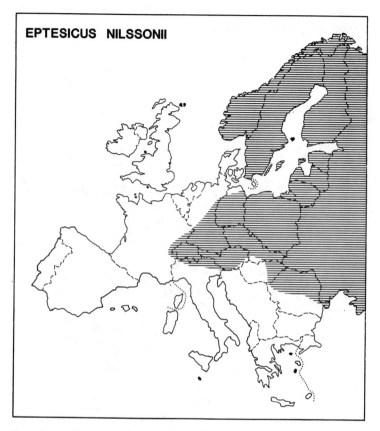

EPTESICUS NILSSONII

Eptesicus nilssonii - **Keyserling & Blasius 1839.**

Size	Forearm length: 38-44mm, Wingspan: 240-280mm, Body mass: 8-16g.
Distribution	From central and eastern Europe east to Iraq and Tibet.
Habitat	An arboreal bat, living in upland areas in the south but lowlands further north. Also roosts in buildings, especially in crevices.
Status	Most abundant bat in north, which appears to be increasing its range.

Vespertilio murinus - **Linnaeus 1758.**

Size Forearm length: 40-47mm, Wingspan: 270-310mm, Body mass: 12-21g.

Distribution From central and eastern Europe through southern Siberia to Afghanistan.

Habitat Found in all types of roosts: buildings, trees and rock crevices, in urban and rural areas.

Status A rare and little-known, migratory bat.

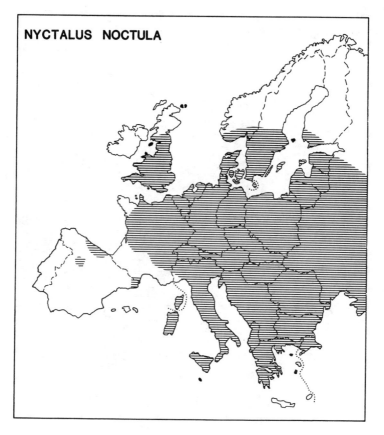

Nyctalus noctula - **Schreber 1774.**

Size	Forearm length: 47-57mm, Wingspan: 320-400mm, Body mass: 17-40g.
Distribution	Most of Europe (excluding Ireland) including Mediterranean islands, east to Japan.
Habitat	Roosts in trees throughout the year, but also occurs in caves and rock crevices, especially in south and east Europe. An arboreal bat preferring to feed around deciduous woodland.
Status	Declining in many areas due to loss of roosts and food. Undertakes long migrations.

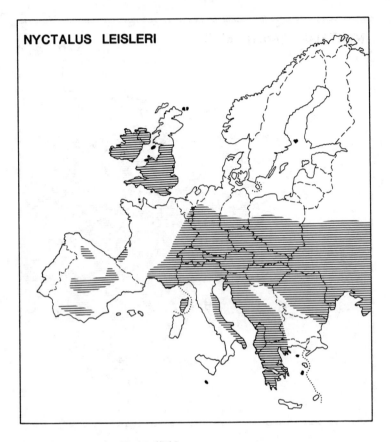

NYCTALUS LEISLERI

Nyctalus leisleri - **Kuhl 1818.**

Size   Forearm length: 38-47mm, Wingspan: 260-320mm,
                  Body mass: 11-20g.

Distribution From western Europe (including Azores and
                  Madeira) to Afghanistan.

Habitat   Nursery colonies found in trees and buildings.
                  Hibernates mostly in trees and rock crevices,
                  occasionally caves. Feeds in open woodland in
                  rural and urban areas.

Status   Rare over most of its range, but abundant in
                  Ireland where large colonies of hundreds are found.

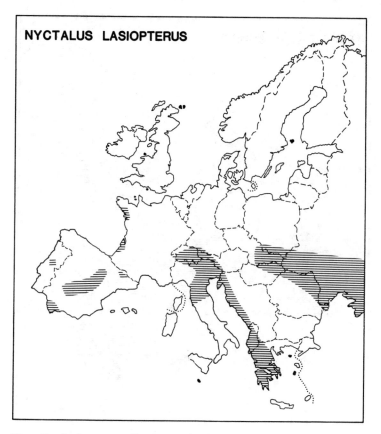

Nyctalus lasiopterus - **Schreber 1780.**

Size   Forearm length: 62-69mm, Wingspan:
                400-460mm, Body mass: 40-75g.

Distribution From western Europe to the Urals and Japan.

Habitat   Little known in Europe. Roosts in trees and
                buildings.

Status   Few scattered records whose populations mostly
                live outside Europe.

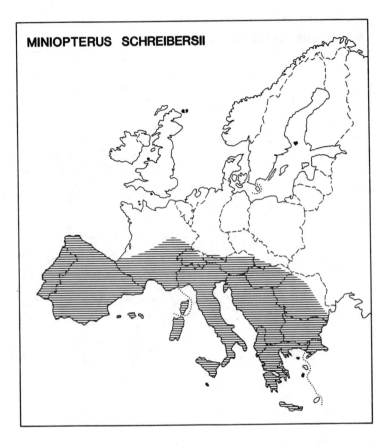

MINIOPTERUS SCHREIBERSII

Miniopterus schreibersii - **Kuhl 1819.**

Size	Forearm length: 43-48mm, Wingspan: 300-340mm, Body mass: 8-16g.
Distribution	Southern Europe, Africa to Japan and Australasia (probably not the same species throughout).
Habitat	Roosts in caves throughout the year in mountainous areas. Occasionally chooses buildings in summer. Feeds in open habitats, but known from scrubby woodlands.
Status	Very large colonies have declined or disappeared due to disturbance. Regarded as endangered. A migratory bat.

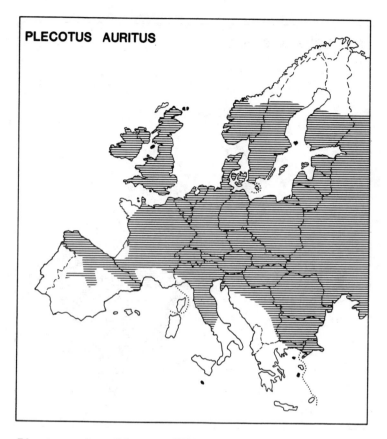

PLECOTUS AURITUS

Plecotus auritus - **Linnaeus 1758.**

Size	Forearm length: 34-42mm, Wingspan: 230-285mm, Body mass: 5-12g.
Distribution	Central and northern Europe, east to Japan.
Habitat	Nursery roosts found in buildings and trees. Hibernates in same sites as well as caves and cellars. Feeds in and around trees both conifer and deciduous.
Status	Many colonies killed by remedial timber treatment in buildings. Also threatened by loss of hollow trees.

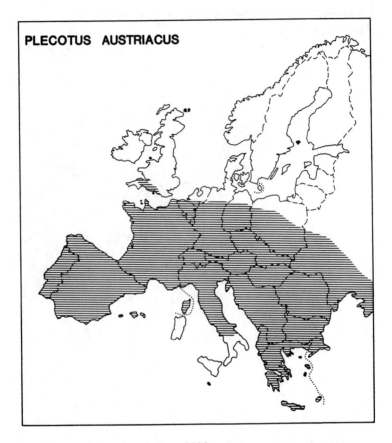

Plecotus austriacus - **Fischer 1829.**

Size	Forearm length: 37-44mm, Wingspan: 255-300mm, Body mass: 7-14g.
Distribution	Central southern Europe and north Africa to west China. Also found on Canary and Cape Verde Islands.
Habitat	Summer roosts occur in lowland buildings and hollow trees. Hibernates in buildings, trees, caves and mines. Feeds mostly in deciduous open woodland.
Status	Vulnerable to remedial timber treatments and loss of hollow trees.

BARBASTELLA BARBASTELLUS

Note: Widespread to 57°N (Latvia) in eastern Baltic States.

Barbastella barbastellus - **Schreber 1774.**

Size	Forearm length: 36-44mm, Wingspan: 245-290mm, Body mass: 6-13g.
Distribution	Western Europe (excluding Ireland and most Scandanavia) east to Caucasus, also Morocco and most large Mediterranean islands.
Habitat	Nurseries mostly in buildings and hollow trees but roosts in exposed sites among leaves and tree roots. Feeds over water and in riparian woodland. Hibernates in caves and tunnels especially in cold.
Status	Rare bat. Colonies destroyed by loss of roosts and remedial timber treatment.

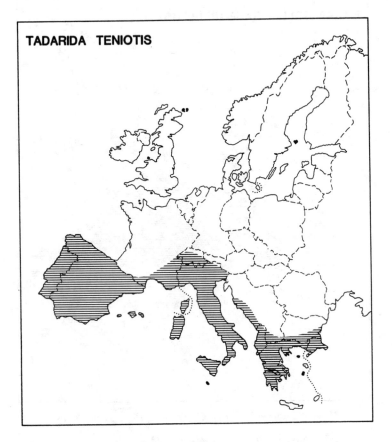

TADARIDA TENIOTIS

Tadarida teniotis - **Rafinesque 1814.**

Size
Forearm length: 57-64mm, Wingspan: 380-420mm, Body mass: 25-50g.

Distribution
Mediterranean Europe including most islands, north Africa through to Japan.

Habitat
Roosts in high buildings, caves and rock crevices, in summer and winter. Fast flying. Feeds high above trees and other obstacles.

Status
Little known. A migratory bat.

Bibliography

- Fenton, M. B., Racey, P. and Rayner, J. M. V. eds. (1987) *Recent advances in the study of bats.* Cambridge University Press, Cambridge.

- Griffin, D. R. (1958) *Listening in the Dark.* Yale University Press, New Haven.

- Kunz, T. H. ed. (1982) *Ecology of bats.* Plenium Press, New York and London.

- Lyster, S. (1985) *International wildlife law.* Grotius Publications, Cambridge.

- Noblet, J. F. (1987) *Les chauves-souris.* Editions Payot, Lausanne.

- Schober, W., and Grimmberger, E (1987) *Die Fledermäuse Europas.* Kosmos-Naturführer, Stuttgart.

- Stebbings, R. E. (1978) Marking bats. In: Stonehouse, B. (ed) *Marking animals.* MacMillan, London.

- Stebbings, R. E. (1986) *Bats.* Anthony Nelson, Oswestry.

- Wimsatt, W. A. ed. (1970) Vols 1 & 2: (1971) Vol 3. *Biology of Bats.* Academic Press, New York.

Useful Addresses

Bat research journals, which contain papers almost exclusively about bat studies in Europe:

'*Nyctalus*' Professor D. Dathe
Tierpark Berlin
1136 BERLIN
Democratic Republic of Germany

'*Myotis*' Zoologisches Forschungsinstitut und
Museum. A. Koenig
Adenauerallee 150-164
D-5300 BONN 1
Federal Republic of Germany

A quarterly newsletter about bats, Great Britain and worldwide:

Fauna and Flora Preservation Society,
c/o Zoological Society of London
Regents Park
LONDON NW1 4RY
England

The Secretariat of the Chiroptera Specialist Group, IUCN Species Survival Commission, is located at the Fauna and Flora Preservation Society, London, (address above).